THE FREELANCER

A Writer's Guide to Success

by

Dennis E. Hensley

and

Stanley Field

    Poetica Press
    5717 Rolling Ridge Rd.
    Indianapolis, IN 46220.

ISBN 0-9613534-0-6

DEDICATION

To all my creative writing workshop people for the flowering of their talent and the stimulation of their ideas.

— STANLEY FIELD

To my wife, Rose, for her love, dedication, dream sharing . . . and financial support during those early years of rejection slips.

— DENNIS E. HENSLEY

ACKNOWLEDGMENTS

Excerpts from *THE WINTER OF OUR DISCONTENT* by John Steinbeck. Copyright 1961 by John Steinbeck. Reprinted by permission of Viking Penguin, Inc.

Excerpts from *THE ART OF FICTION* by W. Somerset Maugham. Copyright 1948, 1954 by W. Somerset Maugham. Reprinted by permission of Doubleday & Company.

Excerpt from *RULE BRITTANIA* by Daphne du Maurier. Copyright 1972 by Daphne du Maurier. Reprinted by permission of Doubleday & Company, Inc.

Excerpt from *"A Worn Path"* by Eudora Welty is reprinted from her volume *A CURTAIN OF GREEN AND OTHER STORIES* by permission of Harcourt Brace Jovanovich, Inc. Copyright 1979.

Excerpt from *THE HUMAN COMEDY* by William Saroyan is reprinted by permission of Harcourt Brace Jovanovich, Inc. Copyright 1943.

Excerpt from *THE FRENCH LIEUTENANT'S WOMAN* by John Fowles, copyright 1969. Reprinted by permission of Little, Brown and Company.

Excerpts from Foreword to *WARM RIVER* and *WARM RIVER* by Erskine Caldwell. Copyright 1932 by Richard Johns, renewed effective 1960 by Erskine Caldwell. Permission for reprint granted by McIntosh and Otis, Inc.

Excerpt from *"Children on Their Birthdays"* from *A TREE OF NIGHT AND OTHER STORIES* by Truman Capote, copyright 1963. Reprinted by permission of Random House, Inc.

Excerpt from *SOPHIE'S CHOICE* by William Styron, copyright 1980. Reprinted by permission of Random House.

ABOUT THE AUTHORS

Dr. Dennis E. Hensley holds four university degrees in English, including a Ph.D. in British and American literature. He is the author of numerous books, including *Positive Workaholism, Staying Ahead of Time* and *Become Famous, Then Rich*. Dr. Hensley has published more than 1,500 freelance articles in such periodicals as *The Writer, Reader's Digest, Essence, Christian Science Monitor, The Cincinnati Enquirer, El Paso Times* and *Detroit Free Press*. He is a regional correspondent for *Writer's Digest,* a monthly columnist in *The Christian Writer,* and a contributing editor for *ShopTalk, The Ball State University Forum, Optical Management,* and *New Fort Wayne Magazine.* Each year he makes more than 30 personal appearances nationwide to teach at writer's conferences, colleges, universities and writers' clubs.

Stanley Field is a successful author, teacher and poet. His poems have appeared in *Northwoods Journal, Green's Magazine* and *World of Poetry Anthology,* among many others. He has taught creative writing at Mount Vernon College and The American University. As a screenwriter, Mr. Field's documentaries have appeared on NBC-TV, WNYU-TV, WMCA radio, WINX radio and WRBN radio. He served as a writer and producer for such television series as "The Big Picture" and such radio series as "Campus Salute." His previous books include *Television and Radio Writing* (Houghton-Mifflin), *The Mini-Documentary* (Tab) and *Guide to Opportunities in the Sciences* (Public Affairs Press).

THE FREELANCER

A Writer's Guide To Success

by **Dennis E. Hensley** and **Stanley Field**

INTRODUCTION

There is an old saying that one cannot be all things to all people. Some readers and/or critics, in noting the table of contents, will probably say that this book is trying to be all things to all people. If so, we admit it. We have our reasons.

In teaching and writing for the past two decades, our creative writing classes and workshops have covered both fiction and nonfiction. Students have submitted short stories, chapters of novels, children's books, science fiction, biographies, articles, outlines and chapters for nonfiction books. Their interests have been as varied as their years.

Each year we travel, individually, nationwide to teach writing workshops, to lecture at writers' conferences and to work as consultants, one-on-one, with novice writers. Many of the problems we are asked to solve are unrelated to grammar, punctuation or writing styles. All too often they relate more to day to day personal problems than those of literary matters: "With two small children to care for, how can I find time to write?" or "How can I be a successful freelance feature writer if I live in a small town?" or "How can I sell the same article to half a dozen different publications?" It is the purpose of this book to provide answers to these and dozens of similar questions.

There are many fine books devoted to one of the many types of writing — the short story, the novel, nonfiction, among others. When we are asked to suggest a text, we usually find it necessary to recommend at least half a dozen books for supplementary reading. That is why the focus of this book is general: to cover all of those practical writing areas offering opportunities for free-lance writers, no matter how varied their interests.

There is another important reason for the diversity of interests represented. Adult education and continuing education classes in creative writing have proliferated. The classes are heterogeneous. The students range in age from mid-twenties to mid-sixties. Evening groups are generally evenly divided between men and women. Among them are beginners who have an urge to write stories; others who have amassed a fund of experience and want to relate those incidents in print; writers who have worked hard and long on articles and stories only to be met with rejection.

This book is designed to be a collection of proven writing tips, and more. Emphasis is on the practical. Theory is important. However, without the ability to apply it, it is worthless. For example, most beginning writers understand the fundamentals of writing. But many never get started because they "can't find the time" to write. That is why "Time Management for Freelance Writers" is the first chapter of this book. This one and the seven that follow provide solid, step-by-step advice designed to get and keep the writer writing.

Robert Louis Stevenson was once asked if he loved to write. He replied, "I hate to write. But, I love to have written." Anyone who has ever tried to work as a freelance writer shares Stevenson's sentiments. It is a joy to see your byline in print, to receive a royalty check in the mail and to get compliments from people who are enthusiastic about the things you have written. However, getting to that stage is difficult.

Writing is one of the oldest of all professions. As such, there is a wealth of recorded experience to draw upon. Novice writers can study the lessons passed on by the more experienced and, in so doing, avoid certain pitfalls. Just as we can learn by doing, we can also learn by reading what others have done.

Epiticus the Greek said two millenniums ago, "If you want to be a writer, write." That's still good advice. In our century, Joseph Pulitzer wrote, "Put it before them briefly so they will read it, clearly so they will appreciate it, picturesquely so they will remember it and, above all, accurately so they will be guided by its light." That, too, is good advice.

We hope this book will serve a need for all those who desire to write, whether they attend a class or not. There are no magic formulas. But a book or a workshop can act as a catalyst, can motivate you, can guide you, and can help you to achieve your goal.

The question is continually raised by people who want to write: Can anyone be taught to write? The answer, based on years of teaching creative writing, is a qualified yes. Techniques can be taught; critiques can be offered; motivation can be provided. But talent?

A conference of teachers of creative writing some years ago at the Library of Congress comes to mind. During one of the panel discussions, a member of the audience asked one of the professors how frank he was with students. "Very frank," the professor responded. "If I don't think students have talent, I tell them so." But then he went on to relate an incident concerning a young married woman who was writing a novel. After reading her work, he told her she would probably be much happier staying at home attending to her children. Obviously, she was unhappy. But about two years later, the professor received a package in the mail. It was a novel the student had written bearing the imprint of a major publisher, and a review praising it highly.

How many neophytes become best-selling writers? First, let us point out, not to be negative but to give you the facts of writing life, that writing for publication is probably the most competitive of all professions. We know of no other profession where so many toil so long for so little. The mass circulation magazines reject as many as three to five *thousand* manuscripts for every one they buy. Only about ten percent of the manuscripts submitted to publishers wind up between book covers. Yet, despite the tremendous competition, the hundreds of thousands of un-published manuscripts written annually, the inordinate amount of rejections, new writers *are* published each year.

Yes, it can be done. We hope this book will help you, in some measure, to achieve that much desired goal of publication.

SF/DH

CHAPTER ONE

TIME MANAGEMENT FOR FREELANCE WRITERS

As writers, we know our language makes use of such expressions as "biding time," "stalling for time" and "buying time." But these are only abstract ideas. They do not alter the fact that the distribution of time is effected with complete equity. All of us have an opportunity to use time efficiently to our own advantage.

Freelance writers are not content with the safe steady incomes of their salaried jobs; they also want big cash advances, regular royalty checks and steady reprint commissions. Writers are highly motivated people who desire to be compensated accordingly. And justly so, since theirs is an extremely challenging profession.

Successful writers have a way of using and controlling their time and know how to value it. A young reporter once asked W. Somerset Maugham how he was able to write so many books, plays and short stories when it was known that he wrote only from nine until noon each day. Replied Maugham, "Son, I write 24 hours a day. I only *type* three hours a day!" Lesson: a real writer knows that *all* time is useful time.

TEN RULES FOR MANAGING TIME

I have had the privilege of interviewing many successful writers. For several years I have also taught at various writers' conferences, where I've worked with successful writers in every phase of creative and professional writing. One thing I've always inquired about has been their systems for managing time. From their responses and from my own experiences, I've found there are ten steps which can be taken to help a person's life and writing career become productive. Let's examine them:

1. Prepare a Life Map

Philosophers refer to a person's years on earth as "the journey down life's road." Although the expression is dull, the symbol within is sharp. Just as one cannot drive from one state to another without a detailed road map, one also cannot advance in a writing career without a detailed life map.

Making a life map is a lot like planning a one-week vacation. Before you leave on vacation, you generally decide upon a destination.

A life map works the same way. You need to sit down and decide what your writing career destinations will be. Where do you want to be a year from now? Five years from now? Twenty-five years from now?

When Thomas Mann was 25 years old, he made a notebook entry to start thinking about a novel based on the Faust theme. When Mann was age 70, he began to write *Dr. Faustus.* Harry Mark Petrakis knew when he was 20 that he wanted to be a writer. He set up a ten-year program of reading and writing. When he was 30, his first story was sold to the *Atlantic Monthly* and was later developed into a screenplay for television's *Dick Powell Theater.* Jack London left the University of California after one semester because he believed he wasn't learning fast enough. He devised a long-range plan of self-study in philosophy, science, literature and history, which had an end goal of helping him to become a writer by age 24. At 24, London's short story collection *A Son of the Wolf* was published.

A writer's personal goals should be fixed in writing. Just knowing what your objective is will help you reach it faster. If you want to become a best-selling novelist, set a target year for that to happen. If you want to become a syndicated columnist, decide now when that can realistically take place. By making these advance decisions, you can determine what will be required (attend more writers' conferences? read a book a week? finish a college degree?) to prepare for your trip to these destinations.

The Life Map shown in the example will not only be a useful tool in helping you to determine where you are going, but it also will give you direct ideas from your own warehouse of mental creativity as to how you can get there.

2

X RETIREMENT

(Write a Who's Who entry about your life and accomplishments)

DATE:

DATE:

MY GOALS:

Thirty Years From Now

DATE:

MY GOALS:

Fifteen Years From Now

DATE:

MY GOALS:

Five Years From Now

DATE:

MY GOALS:

Three Years From Now

DATE:

MY GOALS:

One Year From Now

X STARTING POINT

(Write a summary of your writing accomplishments to date)

DATE:

2. Game-Plan Your 24-Hour Segments

Interviews with successful people in business, science, entertainment and education have shown me that the key trait they all share is their ability to organize. They leave little to chance and are uncomfortable with "winging it." They like order, discipline and specific game-planning. And that is why nearly all of them are perpetual list-makers. Each person lists the work to be done for the day and then systematically digs in to accomplish those objectives.

When a writer uses a daily schedule or daily planner, he or she sees clearly the goals that have been set (those destinations on the Life Map), and it becomes easier for that person to stay on the right track. Furthermore, by listing all the daily chores which must be handled, the individual is able to plan for blocks of time needed for big projects (such as doing research for a long nonfiction book) or time needed for small projects (such as using that last 15 minutes before lunchtime to draft one query letter or return a phone call to a literary agent).

The sample Daily Schedule and Planner has been proven effective and can be modified for any writer's specific needs. Have several hundred copies run off and get into the habit of filling one out before bed each night for use the next day. Ten minutes of planning can save four hours of squandered time. Set weekly, monthly and yearly goals. Write them at the top of the schedule as a constant reminder of the truly important objectives of your career.

Some writers list a newspaper feature that has a Friday deadline as their weekly goal, a national magazine article that must be submitted by the end of the month as their monthly goal, and a book that must be researched by December as their yearly goal. As the goals are written out, they become fixed in the subconscious; before long, they find themselves directing all of their efforts toward achieving those three major goals.

It is also a good idea to make a block on the page in which to delineate your life priorities. Working hard is absurd if it means sacrificing one's family life, one's health, or one's friends. So choose your priorities; write them down and show respect for them.

4

DAILY SCHEDULE AND PLANNER

Today's Date: _____

This Week's Goal: _____

This Month's Goal: _____

This Year's Project: _____

My Life Priorities:	Today's Errands:		Typing To Do:
	Ongoing Research Projects:		
Letters To Write:	Phone Calls To Make:	Appointments And Scheduled Interviews:	Misc.

Also, make a list of errands that must be accomplished. Although writers would naturally like to devote all of their time to writing, things such as getting a haircut, doing the marketing, repairing a child's broken bicycle chain and fixing the lock on the door are chores we all have to face. The best thing to do is to designate so many chores per day to accomplish and then, simply, get them done. Getting these things done will save you at least 20 minutes a day in "nagging" time.

List phone calls and appointments in separate categories. In the phone call block, try to list calls so that the easy ones can be tackled first and the longer, more involved ones can be made as time permits toward the day's end. In the appointment block, list appointments by name and time, such as "interview with Jane Smith, 10:15 A.M."

Have a space to list letters which need to be written. (If you owe your mother a letter, list it, too.) Don't forget that the schedule will be used both at home and at your regular job. Your *entire* day should be planned. *All* your objectives should be listed.

Have a space to list all typing that needs to be done, such as query letters, file information, manuscript drafts, book contract responses and research notes. After each item, pen your initials or those of your typing service so you will know who will be responsible for each typing task.

You will also need a space to remind yourself of ongoing research projects. You may want to reserve your Monday lunch hour for a visit to the library to make photostatic copies of magazine articles related to research for your next book. You might pencil in an hour on Tuesday to work on a draft of a press release about your current book; you can send the press release draft to your publisher for use in long-range publicity efforts. Wednesday night you may wish to schedule some private time to begin to formulate ideas for a speech you'll need to have ready in two months to deliver at the local library association meeting. Anything which involves long-range research or planning should be listed so that it can be worked on a little each week, rather than all at once as the deadline approaches. Remember that crisis management is *no* management.

And, finally, have a miscellaneous space. This can be used to note a dental appointment, a daily exercise period or the weekly meeting of a writers' club.

People who say, "I wonder where the day went!" are not people who have carefully outlined a game plan for their days. Don't you be guilty of that. Design a daily schedule and use it every day!

3. Link Your Tasks

Instead of leaving your writing desk five times a day, arrange your schedule so that five tasks can be done in rapid succession. Pick up the cake at the bakery and drop off your clothes at the cleaners on the way to your 2:00 P.M. interview appointment. After a 45-minute visit, stop at the local school for your 3:15 P.M. meeting with your son's teacher. If five trips (15 minutes out and 15 minutes back) can be reduced to one trip, two hours are saved in travel alone.

Also, think of ways to do simultaneous work. If your shoes need shining, buff them while dictating query letters into a tape recorder and save 20 minutes. If there are magazine articles which need to be read, do so while having the stylist cut your hair and gain 30 minutes for yourself. Keep in mind that the key to good time management is not working harder but, instead, working smarter.

4. Reduce Interruptions

No writer plagued by constant interruptions can be successful. Interruptions need to be controlled. Here are six tips on how to reduce them.

First, learn to say *no* without feeling guilty. If your writing commitments are going to keep you too occupied to accept other responsibilities, make your apologies and bow out. Keep your writing goals in mind, and don't be ashamed to protect the time needed to achieve them by saying no to ancillary activities.

Second, abandon the "open door" policy. Secure a block of private time for yourself each day and do not allow anyone to intrude. If you have to, go to a hideout for an hour (a library or your church's conference room). Two hours of privacy accomplish more than four hours with interruptions.

Third, exert control over your working environment. If your children distract you when they walk in the hall, close the door. If your wife's electric mixmaster breaks your train of thought, ask her not to run it while you are writing (or use the drone of a dehumidifier as "white noise" or an FM radio for a counternoise override). If the interior decor of your home office is brassy and annoying, change it.

Fourth, assemble all supplies before beginning a project. Leaving your writing desk every ten minutes to get files, reference books, notepads or typing paper will not only waste 30 or 40 minutes of valuable time, but also will continually disrupt the intense concentration needed for the writing at hand.

Fifth, plan for a work pause. Most writers feel they need a half-hour coffee break in the morning and afternoon. Nonsense. That amounts to 20 wasted hours per month. Instead, give yourself occasional five-minute breaks for deep breathing exercises, a slow-munching snack, a brisk walk outside or a few moments of relaxed meditation. A short five-minute "breather" usually serves as an adequate change of pace for regenerating the creative thought processes and revitalizing your energy.

Sixth, build a little slack time into the daily routine to handle the inevitable interruption. If you have allowed some flex-time (a shorter lunch hour, some overrun time at day's end), you won't panic if you are ever thrown out of synchronization with your planned events of the day.

The basic lesson here is that interruptions are saboteurs of good time management practices. They must be guarded against, controlled or eliminated.

5. Control the Telephone

As a tool to save steps, trips and time, the telephone can be the writer's best friend. As a chatterbox time-killer, it can be the writer's worst enemy. If you are a time-conscious free-lance writer, you need to be in control of your phone conversations. Let's review a few steps which can help you manage time spent on the phone.

8

Provide your secretary or spouse with three lists of people and instructions on how to screen their calls. The first list will pin-point people you will talk to anytime, such as important editors, publishers, literary agents or your coauthor. The second list will note people to whom you will talk during routine work or home hours, but not when you are concentrating on a special writing project. These people may include service club presidents, certain relatives or your writing colleagues. The third list will focus on people you do not wish to talk to, such as politicians seeking donations, long-winded friends or random phone solicitors. Your family members or secretary can serve as sieves filtering your calls; only the important business-related calls should reach you. Struggling writers may find this difficult to do at first, but stay with it. In a few days you'll be convinced of its merit.

Next, you must learn to set the tone when you want phone calls to be brief. Saying, "What can I do for you?" is more effective than "It's good to hear from you again." Be courteous, but keep the conversation in line with its purpose. Curtail it as soon as possible. If necessary, buy a three-minute egg timer and turn it over when your phone rings. When the sand runs out, make an effort to end the conversation. Five daily phone conversations reduced from 10 to three minutes gains you 35 minutes. (If you find it difficult to end conversations, you might consider having a telephone amplifier installed in your home or office so you can be working at your file cabinet or bookcase while still talking.)

Finally, reduce incoming calls by initiating necessary calls yourself and getting them behind you. Also, suggest specific times when people should return calls to you. This will put people on your time schedule, not vice versa.

Freelance writers should not be comfortable "shooting the breeze" over the phone during working hours. That can be done at parties or on television talk shows after one has written a best-seller. Writing hours are hours for writing. Remember that the next time you pick up a telephone receiver.

6. Set and Follow Deadlines

In the publishing business, nothing is more important than meeting the deadline. The word — deadline — explains the whole

9

situation: go past this line and you're dead. Freelance writers must set and follow self-imposed deadlines. Evaluate how much time you will need to complete a project; then see to it that it is finished by or before that time.

Finishing ahead of a deadline is a display of excellent time management. You know how it is with bank loans: pay off a loan one month ahead of time and you will earn yourself an A-1 credit rating; pay off the loan one month behind time and you will be labeled a "bad risk." The same goes for writing. If you have promised to supply a magazine editor a 4,000-word feature and you deliver your article five days early rather than one day late, you will make a very favorable impression.

Your Life Map and your Daily Planner list goals according to self-imposed deadlines of one day, one week, one month, one year and many years to come. Make these deadlines challenging. Adhere to them. Keep in mind that you are not running in a pack, nor are you in a race against any other particular writer. Your race is against a timepiece, not another person. Only you know what you should be "clocking at the first turn" in order to finish in record time.

7. Don't Procrastinate

Novelist Wright Morris told *Publishers' Weekly* in 1979, "A regimen is absolutely crucial to a writer. Much of a writer's inspiration derives from this: you write — and you find you have something to say."

Stalling, delaying and procrastinating are not techniques employed by writers who care about good time management. Instead, serious writers force themselves to report to their writing desks at specified times, whether or not they are in the mood to write.

Getting started is seldom easy. It takes discipline. Facing that blank piece of paper can be gruesome, but the dedicated writer will not turn away from it. Waiting for the muse to strike is an amateur's excuse.

Different writers have used different incentives or punishments to get themselves started at their writing. Maugham would report to his writing desk at 9:00 A.M. sharp; if nothing creative came to mind, he would start to write his name over and over until the motion of the pen got him into a writing mood. Similarly, when E. B. White drew a mental blank, he would purposely write the most ridiculous sentence he could think of ("Juggling parakeets is my deaf uncle's hobby") and then engage his mind for a few minutes in developing a silly supportive story to go with the topic sentence. Once creatively "in gear," he would turn to more serious writing.

Alexandre Dumas believed in writing in marathon stints in order to make use of creativity while it was flowing. It is said he once finished writing a novel, wrote "The End" in midpage, and then began a new novel on the blank lower half of that same page. Ernest Hemingway worked in an opposite manner. Hemingway would stop writing right in the middle of a battle scene, love scene or passage of dialogue; the next day, when he returned to his writing, he knew right where to pick it up, and thus he was able to proceed with reaching his daily quota of writing.

Nathaniel Hawthorne's strict Puritan heritage gave him a mild guilt complex over earning money "simply" from writing; to relieve his guilt and free his thinking processes, he would *stand* all the while he was writing. By comparison, Mark Twain had to stretch out in bed (and light up a big black cigar) before he could write. Neither Hawthorne nor Twain shunned his writing responsibilities.

Jack London was another writer who did not believe in procrastination. London began to write at age 18. He died of uremic poisoning at age 40. In that short span of 22 years, London produced 190 short stories, 22 novels, and more than 600 major items of journalism (from front-line coverage of the Russo-Japanese War to ringside reports on the Jeffries-Johnson title bout). He did so by not leaving his writing room until he had written 1,000 words of salable copy each day.

When Jack London was asked in a letter from Cloudesley Johns (an aspiring writer) what a novice writer should do to advance his career, London wrote back, "Don't loaf and invite inspiration; light out after it with a club, and if you don't get it you will nonetheless get something that looks remarkably like it. Work all the time!"

The underlying success factors in each of these writers' careers were discipline, persistence and the determination to work even when they didn't feel overly motivated.

8. Tap Your Biorhythm Peak

In recent years scientists have offered us results of biorhythm studies as proof of something many of us knew all along: different people work best at different times of the day. Anthony Trollope wrote from 5:00 to 8:00 A.M. each day before going to his civil service job. Jules Verne was an insomniac who wrote novels at night. Sir Arthur Conan Doyle wrote early in the morning while still dressed in slippers and a robe. We all peak at different times.

I am one of those writers who come alive at night. When the television set is turned off, the kids are in bed, the noises outdoors cease and the blackness of night hides all ancillary distractions, I turn on. I retreat to my office, I pick up a pencil and some paper and I begin to write. From 10:00 P.M. until 2:00 A.M. I am at my creative peak. No one disturbs me; nothing interrupts me. I usually can produce 1,500 words of polished copy, as opposed to half that much when writing from 10:00 A.M. until 2:00 P.M. And, by writing at night, I do not take time away from my wife and family.

To tap the power of your own prime time, ask yourself which two consecutive hours (6:00 to 8:00 A.M.? noon to 2:00 P.M.? 9:00 to 11:00 P.M.?) you enjoy most and feel your best. You may want to chronicle your hour-by-hour activities for a few days to help gauge your peak time of strength and efficiency. Structure your work so that the most important challenges will face you then. Do not use prime time hours for reading the newspaper, making phone calls or watching television. Use these hours for planning a short story, writing a book outline or tackling some other challenging mental task.

Part of good time management calls for an analysis of the quality of the various hours of your day. Use your prime time for your prime tasks.

9. Learn to Delegate Work

Being able to decide which tasks to tackle personally and which to delegate is important. If you pass along work (routine typing, proofreading) to a competent person who can get the job done right, you will save numerous hours of time. If you give a job to anyone who happens to be handy and the work is improperly carried out, you can create a double workload for yourself.

When to delegate work can be determined by asking yourself three questions:

1. *Can this task be delegated or am I the only person qualified to do it properly?* For example, if you are researching a book on German history, you'll have to decide whether or not your co-author, secretary or assistant is qualified to do library research work or whether, to get it correct, you'll need to do it yourself.

2. *If I delegate this task, will it take me longer to explain what needs to be done than it would for me just to do it myself?* For instance, you could type and mail a filler faster than you could teach someone how to set it up and type it in correct manuscript format. Likewise, you could make some calls on your own and get a faster reply than making a list of points for someone else to ask about when he or she called for you.

3. *Does this task involve any confidential writing or publication plans which I should not bring someone else in on?* For example, when I was granted an exclusive interview with Walter and Charlotte Baldwin (the mother- and father-in-law of the Rev. Jim Jones) shortly after the Jonestown, Guyana, massacre, they requested that the interview not be published for at least six months so that the furor could lessen somewhat. To prevent against press leaks, the transcription of notes and manuscript typing were done by myself and I used no literary agent or other third party when contacting editors about publication plans.

When you do delegate a task, don't "oversupervise" it. Set a schedule, make regular progress checks and never allow a delegated task to be handed back to you unfinished. For example, if you hire a college student to type the final draft of your 400-page novel, tell the typist you will want the manuscript ready in 40 days, that you will come by every 10 days to pick up 100 pages for proofreading and that you will pay for the work when the entire project has been completed. With this arrangement, you'll maintain control of the work without actually having to do it.

10. Avoid Burnout

Just as machines need periodic rests and regular maintenance in order to produce at top levels, so do freelance writers. Fatigue, whether mental or physical, slows you down and drains your time.

To avoid physical fatigue, get away from the desk long enough to get some substantial exercise. Remember also to eat a balanced diet (not just a cup of coffee at arm's length and a quick doughnut between pencil sharpening pauses).

To avoid mental fatigue you can read a stimulating book. Also, be sure to plan some quiet time for yourself; remember to infuse laughter into your life; find time to accept offerings of love and praise from friends and family; and occasionally indulge in some change-of-pace activities.

Whenever novelist Thomas Hardy felt mentally fatigued, he would leave his pen and paper and slip off to a nearby pub for a couple of games of darts with the village locals. When writer Erskin Caldwell felt mentally fatigued, he would put down his pencil and pick up a dictionary and start to read about words. Whatever form of brief diversion you favor, use it to keep yourself mentally keen.

Let's reflect for a moment on what we've learned thus far. We discovered that people relate to time in different ways and that people actually function best at certain times of day. We all have an equal amount of time which we can either squander, use conservatively or invest wisely for maximum return. Such practices as planning our day's work on paper, delegating tasks to assistants, making a plan for our lives, curbing daily interruptions and learning not to procrastinate can make major positive changes in our lives.

FOUR RULES FOR OVERCOMING REJECTION

Earlier we talked about the need to guard against mental fatigue. One of the principal reasons writers do suffer from fatigue and depression is because they find it difficult to handle rejection. When query letters and manuscripts come back in the mail with printed rejection slips attached, many writers experience the "freelancer's blues." Some writers avoid the writing desk or typewriter for days at a time as they mull over their imagined failure and incompetence. This is a tragic waste of time.

The fact is that rejection is a lifelong part of the writer's life. The fact that I still receive rejection slips is hard for people who know me to grasp. I run writing workshops and give guest lectures at more than two dozen universities and writing clubs each year. Because my byline has appeared hundreds of times in many of the leading publications in this country, my students think that selling manuscripts is no problem for me. But they are wrong.

The truth is that in freelance writing each new presentation is judged on its own merits; and if it's not what the editor wants, it gets rejected.

And that hurts.

We all hate rejections. We don't care how they are worded — nicely or bluntly — we *hate* rejections. That's probably why we do everything possible to avoid them. To help soften the blow of rejection when it comes, here are four basic rules to follow.

1. Job Identity

Understand your job and what it entails; and if you cannot face up to its negative aspects, don't get involved in it.

When I was a college freshman, I got it into my head that I wanted to be a writer. My concept of a writer was that of someone who picked up a notepade, traveled to exotic places, met interesting people, wrote about his or her discoveries and made a lot of easy money. Years later I learned that a writer is really someone who bangs on a secondhand typewriter, seldom gets out of town, meets a few interesting people and makes an amount of money in direct proportion to the hours of hard work he or she puts in.

I wasted several good years as I dabbled in journalism, play-writing and fiction, running into brick walls everywhere while I sought my identity as some kind of writer. So, look the job of writing squarely in the eye, roll up your sleeves and remember that, like any other job, writing requires a lot of hard work and determination.

2. Quantity vs. Quality

Do your research, prepare a quality manuscript and don't judge your productivity by volume alone.

Another problem I had as a beginning freelance writer was that I believed that persistence would be rewarded on its own merit. For two years I wrote manuscripts like a man possessed. I'd write, type and mail an article a day for days on end.

My only rewards for this marathon writing stint were 57 used manila envelopes, several dollars in cancelled stamps, sore typing fingers . . . and my first 57 rejection slips.

In my third year I learned to carefully study a target publication to determine things like writing style, audience, article length, editorial guidelines and use of photos. I also spent more time on my writing. I edited, reviewed, revised, rewrote and retyped whole pages four or five times. That year my sales more than tripled.

3. Educational Preparation

Read, study and thoroughly research the field of writing, as well as the subject areas about which you wish to write, so that your editors will have faith in you.

Perhaps the greatest flaw in my thinking as a young writer was the belief that anyone could write professionally. After all, I reasoned, I had been writing since second grade. It was simple. I had talent. My teachers always complimented me on my penmanship, and my grandmother was forever telling people that I wrote her lovely letters.

So, I dashed off a couple of short stories and a few articles and waited for my royalty checks to arrive. It was a three-year wait. And I was only successful then because I had taken some college courses in journalism, had read more than 30 books on how to write and had spent more years practicing my writing skills.

Writing is a skill. The more you practice it, the better you become at it. Along with that goes the study one must give to the subject being presented. A writer cannot turn out a 2,000-word manuscript on something he or she hasn't researched.

4. Follow-up

Pursue new markets, but keep in close contact with your established markets.

A simple mistake I made as a novice writer was to look continually for new markets. I later learned that once an editor had accepted one of my articles, I had a foot in the door. It was easy to return to a magazine where my writing and research abilities were already established. This saved time, cut red tape and increased my income quickly.

Many times writing students will lament, "I'm beginning to think it's not worth it. There are just too many rejections in this business. It's too hard. Everyone else I talk to has the same problem."

I get excited at such a self-defeated attitude and I seek to explain, "That is what is so wonderful about rejection. This would not be a challenging occupation if the continuous grapple with rejection didn't exist. Nor would this field be so accessible and lucrative. Sure, everyone gets rejected — even the top pros. But be glad about that. It shows that if you are well prepared, your chance is as strong as anyone's for success!"

Rejection is something we should see as a potentially positive factor. Don't let it discourage you.

SPEEDING YOUR CAREER ALONG:
THE WRITER'S CONFERENCE

The key time management question asked by most freelance writers is, "How can I transform from a novice to a professionally competent writer in the shortest amount of time?" My response to

17

that is: get help from writers who are already successful. The best way to do that is to attend one or more of the dozens of writers' conferences held in the United States each year.

As a fledgling freelance writer, I floundered on my own for three years before attending my first five-day writers' conference. The three years were poorly spent; the five days were well invested. After that first conference, my writing career began to move forward.

Today, I still attend conferences, but now it is as an instructor. Nevertheless, I still find the same value and excitement in conferences which I found many years ago when I, too, was first starting to write. When it comes to meeting interesting people, gathering fresh writing ideas, discovering new publishing markets, becoming familiar with different styles and formats of writing, or just getting away for some enjoyable travel, nothing matches a well-planned writing conference.

Unfortunately, very few people know how to make the best use of time at a writers' conference. Getting your money's worth out of a conference is like getting your money's worth out of a vacation: it takes careful selection and advance planning and preparation.

Begin by selecting a conference best suited to your needs. Decide this by asking friends and fellow writers about the conferences they have attended and by writing to several conference directors for free descriptive brochures. Usually, by figuring in advance how much money you will have to spend on travel and tuition, you will be able to narrow the choices rapidly. Study the conference programs for content (there should be plenty of lectures by reputable instructors) and emphasis (some conferences offer something for everyone, whereas others focus strictly upon travel writing or poetry or fiction).

Don't rule out a conference several hundred miles from home. If you are a working writer — even a beginner — your expenses may be tax deductible. Furthermore, you may be able to write travel features about the location you'll be visiting. The most important consideration is to get the kind of help you need for your particular writing interest. Invest in yourself in order to improve your writing, and you stand a good chance of increasing your manuscript sales.

It is, I think, not advisable to attend the same conference more than two years in a row. Not everyone will agree with this assessment, however. Some people feel "comfortable" in familiar surroundings and among old acquaintances. My feeling, however, is that the enthusiasm at conferences comes from studying under new teachers, visiting different places, and discovering new programs. Exposure to new people and areas is the best experience writers can give themselves.

Once you've selected a conference, be sure to go to it with all necessary materials in hand. Bring pencils, pens, a notebook, typing paper, a portable typewriter (if traveling by car), a tape recorder and microphone, if possible, for lectures and interviews with guest authors out of class, plus extra cassette tapes and batteries.

When packing your camera, bring along a spare battery, both black-and-white and color film (travel editors usually want one or two color photos of any place you write about), a flash unit (extra batteries for it, too), and a small notepad to jot down the locations in the photos as you shoot them.

Bring a book or two to read during the evenings, when you are trying to wind down after a hectic day of classes and workshops.

Most important, bring along at least three of your manuscripts. Some conferences arrange informal swap-and-critique sessions at which the conference registrants read and analyze each other's manuscripts. You probably will also have a private counseling session with one of the conference instructors, and he or she will want to examine your writing. Since many editors of leading magazines "drop in" at conferences, you may have a chance to put your article or short story directly into the hands of someone you've had trouble reaching by mail.

When you arrive at the conference, be quick about "working the crowds." Look at name tags and find people from other states. Ask them about their regional publications, about the freelance policies of the large newspapers in their states, and about any writing workshops or conferences coming up in their areas.

If you are looking for a coauthor for a book or article, place a not on the workshop bulletin board immediately upon your arrival. Explain the project and list your home and temporary conference addresses.

During breakfast or lunch on the first day, strike up a conversation with someone who will be attending classes you won't. Offer to trade the notes from your classes on poetry and playwriting, for example, for his or her notes from the classes on short story and novel writing.

If it is allowed, tape record the conference lectures. Tapes miss nothing; with the tape "taking notes" (which you can play back over and over once you are home), your mind is free to concentrate on the lecture, questions raised by members of the class, and notations or charts on the blackboard. Also, the tape allows you to write memos, such as follow-up questions to ask the instructor after class, while the lecture is underway.

When attending your private session with the instructor, be businesslike and thorough. Bring a list of questions about things he or she has said in class for which you need clarification. Also, bring a manuscript and some questions about it.

Be specific. Ask, "How can I improve my dialogue sequence on page nine?" or "Can you help me rework my lead paragraph so that it will have a better narrative hook?" Ask the instructor to help correct those places in the manuscript that have never worked out in rewrites. To help sell the manuscript, draft a sample query letter about it and have the instructor read that, too.

Sometimes private sessions with the instructor can be stretched by making a follow-up appointment of a social nature. Just say, "If you're free between lectures tomorrow afternoon, I'd like to buy the coffee and talk a little more about how you outline books before writing them." Most instructors never tire of "talking shop" and usually will be happy to accept such invitations.

Attending a conference calls for strategy and advance planning in order to take advantage of all that is available. Go to a conference with the goal of gaining enough information to keep you busy for several months, and you'll come away with more than imagined in ideas, contacts, and experiences.

Again, let us pause to review what we have discovered. We have learned that no matter where we are we can still be careful monitors of our time. We also learned that rejection can be a major source of depression and time loss for the writer, but there are ways of dealing with and overcoming rejection. We further learned that attending writers' conferences can offer the writer numerous opportunities for career advancement.

All right, the clock is still ticking. How are *you* going to invest the next 24 hours? One of the most productive ways would be to read the next chapter, which deals with the legal questions about which a writer should be aware.

— Dennis E. Hensley

CHAPTER TWO

LEGAL ASPECTS OF PROFESSIONAL WRITING

"Write about what you know" sounds like a reasonable guideline for authors. Does that mean write about whom you know? A great many first novels are to some degree autobiographical, or about people writers may know intimately. Curiosity is an attribute of writers. They want to know what makes people react as they do. They listen to gossip about a neighbor and a story is envisioned. But can writers actually use their neighbors as characters in their stories?

INVASION OF PRIVACY

In 1890, Louis Brandeis, who was to become one of our most noted Supreme Court justices, wrote a history-making essay, "The Right to Privacy," in collaboration with Sam Warren. The principle expressed in that essay has over the years influenced lawyers, justices and lawmakers; and today it greatly affects writers.

For example, Thomas Wolfe, author of *Look Homeward, Angel* and *You Can't Go Home Again,* devoted much of his writing to scenes set in his hometown of Asheville, North Carolina. The problem was that he was overly realistic. He portrayed the people he knew in Asheville so that they were immediately recognizable, and he was rash enough to use actual names. As a result, his publisher was besieged by invasion of privacy suits that had to be adjudicated at a cost to the publisher of some $40,000. That was a large sum for the 1930s.

Probably the most quoted case involved Marjorie Kinnan Rawlings' novel *Cross Creek.* It was based on an actual person who was a very unusual woman. Although the protagonist was portrayed in a highly favorable light, she sued for invasion of privacy. The judge ruled that indeed her privacy was invaded but since no harm was done, as a matter of fact just the reverse, he awarded her only one dollar in damages. Still, the publisher had to pay legal costs.

Unless you have the written permission of the people involved, it can be hazardous to base fictional characters on real people who are readily recognizable or who are so unique that there can be no question of identification.

However, it should be noted that public print sources used by a writer are not considered an invasion of privacy. For instance, some years ago there was a network docudrama series called *The Big Story*. One of the episodes dealt with the capture and imprisonment of a man who had the unenviable reputation of being the most expert safecracker in the country. The network episode was based on stories about him that had appeared in the public press. It so happened that when the man was released from prison, he went straight and established himself as a businessman in the community in which he now resided. Shortly afterward one of the local television stations scheduled reruns of *The Big Story* episodes. When the reformed criminal saw his repeat episode on the air, he sued for invasion of privacy, but the judge ruled against him on the grounds that all the material used in the broadcast had originally appeared in public print.

LIBEL

Libel is any written or printed statement tending to expose a person to public ridicule or contempt or to injure his or her reputation in any way.

In the case of *Bindrim vs. Davis,* Gwen Davis, a popular novelist, received a contract from her publisher to write a novel based on her experience in group therapy. When the book was published, the doctor who ran the sessions sued on grounds of libel. He argued that even though the writer had camouflaged her story, her unfavorable description of the doctor and his methods could damage his reputation; he was, after all, the only doctor in the United States who provided that type of group therapy, so there could be no question of his identity. The jury awarded him $75,000. The publisher in turn tried to recover that money and the costs involved by filing a lawsuit against the author. Publishers contracts contain an indemnity clause which may read as follows: "That the Work is innocent and contains no matter that is scandalous, obscene or libelous or otherwise contrary to law or injurious to any person." In the Davis case, the conflict between

23

publisher and author was settled by arbitration; the terms were not made public.

Lest the above make you fearful of approaching your typewriter, let me assuage your apprehensions. In the June-July (1981) issue of the *Authors Guild Bulletin,* there was a report of a survey made by the Guild on libel and invasion of privacy suits and claims involving publishers' indemnity clauses. The survey indicated that only a very few of the authors responding had been sued for libel or invasion of privacy (two percent) or had claims asserted against them that were disposed of before suit (1.5 percent).

Most of the lawsuits were not tried: nine were withdrawn and twelve were settled by some payment to the plaintiffs. None of the cases that were decided in court ended in a judgment against the author and publisher. Twenty-seven authors, two percent of those responding, reported 29 suits for libel, invasion of privacy or both, involving 28 books. There were 19 libel suits, four privacy suits and six suits for libel and invasion of privacy. Novels were involved in five cases, nonfiction books in 24.

Note that the overwhelming number of suits involved nonfiction books, mainly unauthorized biographies about politicians or entertainers. Information about these public figures comes mostly from already published sources, which are not always wholly accurate, and from acquaintances of the subject. The biography might include inaccurate or false statements, which could lead to the bringing of a suit by the person being written about. Investigative reports, unless thoroughly corroborated, might contain allegations that lend themselves to complaint and possible libel.

However, if a story or an article or a book is based on someone who is dead, there can be no grounds for invasion of privacy or libel, if your facts are correct. There have been suits involving dead persons. When a book was published on Rasputin after his death, depicting him as an evil force, his heirs sued. The ruling went against the heirs.

PLAGIARISM

Webster's New World Dictionary defines plagiarism as "the appropriation or the imitation of the language, ideas, and thoughts of another author, and representation of them as one's original work."

Under our laws, all published and unpublished works that have been copyrighted are protected against plagiarism. If, for example, you send a manuscript to a publisher, who rejects it, and then you later discover that the publisher has issued a book using your words or ideas verbatim, that could constitute plagiarism. As is true of invasion of privacy and libel, cases of plagiarism are few and far between. When they do occur, they sometimes make headlines, especially if a best-seller is involved.

One would be hard-pressed to find any purely "original" work. Shakespeare, as is well known, obtained some of his finest ideas from *Holinshed's Chronicles.* However, what he did with those histories made all the difference. When you write a short story, a novel, a nonfiction book, what you will probably come up with is a variation on an established theme, and the variations are endless. There are thousands of variations on the Romeo and Juliet theme. One that comes readily to mind is the Arthur Laurents/Leonard Bernstein musical *West Side Story.*

What constitutes plagiarism? Simply stated, plagiarism is the using of the actual words of another author in your manuscript *quantitatively.* I emphasize quantitatively because in works of fiction or nonfiction it is permissible to quote another author briefly or to use portions of a poem or a song lyric to identify an era, let us say. It is not plagiarism to use entire sections of a book which is in the public domain. Currently, public domain generally applies to publications that are more than 56 years old, and were copyrighted under the old law.

Unique problems can arise from using historic source material. Usually, such material is in the public domain and therefore available to any writer. I recall engaging in historical research and coming upon incidents in American Indian lore which I believed would make a fine historical novel. I wrote a synopsis and several chapters and submitted them to a major publisher. By a rare coincidence, that publisher responded that he had already contracted with another author for a book on exactly the same subject. It was, of course, possible to send the manuscript to another publisher, but prior publication of the other book would certainly limit sales. There was, obviously, no plagiarism involved in the foregoing, just coincidence.

Consider, nevertheless, the numerous biographies written about famous personages. The next time you are in the library note how many biographies there are of Lincoln or Washington or Jefferson. It is evident that the basic facts about a famous figure's life, such as birthplace, schools attended, marriages, and so on are available to any researcher, but publishers want some new aspect of the subject explored. Fawn Brodie, in yet another book about Jefferson, succeeded by delving into sexual relations that were either not explored in depth previously or are matters of controversy.

Probably the most arrant case of outright plagiarism occurred when a convict sent a book manuscript to a publisher. The editors at the publishing house were very enthused about the book, even more so when they learned the author was serving a long prison sentence. The publicity would be invaluable. However, one of the editors was disturbed about the book. He asked for a delay in making a final decision and spent a sleepless night worrying about it. Then it came to him. He made a hurried trip to the library, borrowed a book and checked it against the manuscript. They tallied word for word. What had happened was that the convict had borrowed the book from the prison library and proceeded to type it page for page and then shipped it off to the publisher under his own name!

CAMOUFLAGE

When writing nonfiction, one must obviously stick to the facts. There should be no distortions of the truth. But fiction deals in exaggerations. If your story is based on living people, it may be expedient to change the locale: if the real-life incidents took place in a suburb of New York, why not place the fictionalized version in a suburb of Philadelphia? The physical appearance and occupations of your protagonists, unless absolutely essential to the plot, could be changed. Clever camouflage can be a safeguard for the author.

NAMING NAMES

There is another pertinent element writers should consider, and that involves choice of names for fictional characters. Fiction writers may believe that it is best to invent outlandish names which no one is likely to posses. But that device may also have its pitfalls. Witness the prolific mystery writer who had a Chinese laundryman as the villain of one of his books. The locale was Chicago. The writer chose what he considered was a unique name for his villain, but it turned out that there was one Chinese laundryman in all of Chicago with that name. The laundryman sued on the grounds that the book was a source of great embarrassment for him.

In the matter of names, it is probably wiser to check a telephone directory and choose a name (other than John Smith) that appears frequently. Fifty Daniel Gold's, for example, could not sue on the basis of unique name recognition.

COPYRIGHTS

It is not my intention here to delve into the history of copyrights or to explore the fine points of the copyright law which may rarely affect a writer. I do, however, want to include such information as will be of value and assistance to most writers. If the copyright law and all its regulations fascinate you, you can consult two or three books extant which go into great detail, or you can write to the Copyright Office for a copy of the current regulations.

What do writers really need to know about copyrights?

First of all, the current copyright law went into effect on January 1, 1978. Prior to 1978, a copyright could be held for 28 years with a renewal for another 28 years. Under the current law, the author receives copyright protection for the duration of his life plus 50 years. Also, under the old law, plays could be copyrighted before publication or performance but novels could not. Under the new law, one can copyright almost any type of manuscript.

What is the advantage of copyrighting an unpublished manuscript? Perhaps if you are planning a series of stories or books that deal with the adventures of a unique character or have a proposal for a television series, it would be advisable to copyright your manuscript. For registration forms which contain detailed instructions on the registration procedure and number of copies of the work that must accompany the registration form, write to: United States Copyright Office, Library of

Congress, Washington, DC 20559. At this writing, the fee is $10 per registration.

In most instances, books, stories and articles are copyrighted by the publisher. The copyright should be in the author's name, but a few book publishers obtain the copyright in their corporate name. In those cases, authors may request that the copyright be reissued in their own names.

Under common law, a manuscript may be protected even if not copyrighted. For example, if an agent is handling your manuscript or if you are submitting directly to publishers, you should have correspondence which will show the date of your submission.

PERMISSIONS

The "fair use" doctrine is spelled out in Section #107 of Public Law 94-553, the Copyright Act which went into effect in January 1978. Section #107 states:

> The fair use of a copyrighted work, including such use by reproduction in copies or phonorecords or by any other means specified by that section (Section #105), for purposes such as criticism, comment, news reporting, teaching (including multiple copies for classroom use), scholarship, or research, is not an infringement of copyright. In determining whether the use made of a work in any pacticular case is a fair use the factors to be considered shall include:
>
> (1) the purpose and character of the use, including whether such use is of a commercial nature or is for nonprofit educational purposes;
>
> (2) the nature of the copyrighted work;
>
> (3) the amount and substantiality of the portion used in relation to the copyrighted work as a whole; and
>
> (4) the effect of the use upon the potential market for or value of the copyrighted work.

Where excerpts are extensively used, as for example in text-books, and permission fees may have to be paid, some publishers may make advances available to cover the fees either outright or against royalties. In many cases, the copyright owners are willing to give written permission for proper acknowledgment. After all, if your book is at all successful, it will bring the work of the author you quote to the attention of your readers. When formal permission is needed, be sure to get it in writing. Keep the original letter of permission and send a copy to your publisher.

If you are in a position to write a nonfiction book or a textbook which may require extensive material from other writers, you will have to carry on a voluminous correspondence to obtain permissions. In preparing a text on writing for television, I needed to include sample scripts of various television programs. It would have been much too costly if a fee was required to reprint each of the scripts. The letters requesting permission had to be couched in terms that would elicit a favorable response from the television producers. The letter stressed the educational nature of the book. Most of the television producers were very cooperative in supplying scripts and granting permission for reprint.

I have found that the granting of permission to use excerpts varies from publisher to publisher. Some publishers will grant free use of quotations up to 175 words, provided due credit is given to author and publisher. (Such credits are usually listed under Acknowledgments in the front of the book.) Other publishers may require fees of $20 and $25 for even a stanza of two lines. There is no rule of thumb. If you need to use a quotation, unless it is from a book in the public domain, be sure to request permission from the publisher.

CONTRACTS

When a publisher agrees to publish your book, you will be involved with a contract. Many of the provisions of the contracts from major publishers will be similar, but each publisher will have some variants. All contracts will provide for royalty payments, subsidiary rights, acceptance of the manuscript, revisions, advances, warranties and indemnities, and authors' copies.

If authors negotiate their own sale, they would be well advised to have their contract checked by a lawyer. If the authors have an agent, they can generally rely on the agent for advice.

In the matter of sales of manuscripts to periodicals, the formality of a contract will depend on the periodical. If it is a large circulation national magazine, you may receive a formal contract for your manuscript. If it is a literary magazine, religious magazine or regional magazine, you may receive a contract that consists of perhaps a couple of paragraphs in which you warrant that your manuscript is original with you and affirming that the magazine has the right to publish it. Another paragraph will set forth the amount to be paid for the manuscript. Some smaller magazines may ask for all rights. My advice, if that appears in any contractual agreement, is to cross out all rights and insert one time only or First North American Serial Rights and initial the change. Some of the little magazines will send a check, usually on or after publication and write on the check, First North American Serial Rights, which will suffice as your contract.

Most magazines do not request other than first publication rights. Thus, if a short story of yours is sold to a major magazine and subsequently is sold to television, the proceeds of the television sale would be entirely yours; or if a publisher reads your article in a magazine and then commissions you to expand it into a nonfiction book, the contractual arrangements would be between you and the publisher.

In the event that you sell an article to a regional magazine and the article has an appeal to readers of another regional magazine that is noncompetitive, you can resell the article. Several short stories I have written which originally appeared in U.S. publications have been sold subsequently to foreign periodicals. You can see why it is important never to sign away all rights.

You read in the literary gossip columns about the fantastic sums that some authors receive as advances. Remember that these columns or other newspaper stories deal with the sensational, and that there are top-selling writers. You have to realize that million-dollar advances are the happy lot of a very, very few writers.

To be realistic, here is an actual breakdown for a first novel written by one of my students and published as a hardback by Scribner's. The novel, first of all, was sold by an agent. The author received a $2,500 advance against royalties. Since his submission was a completed manuscript, the advance was payable on the signing of the contract. The royalty payments were established as follows: 10 percent on the first 5,000 copies sold, 12½ percent on the next 5,000 and 15 percent on all copies sold in excess of 10,000. These are the minimum terms that an author should accept.

With a major publisher the royalties should be based on the retail price; that is, if the book is listed at $10, the author receives $1 for each of the first 5,000 copies sold and then upward on the sliding scale. Some smaller publishers who do not have the capital of their larger competitors will base royalties on the net received by the publisher. For example, if the book is listed at $10 but the publisher receives a net of $6, he will contract with the writer to receive sixty cents rather than one dollar on each book sold, and there may not be any sliding scale at all.

Most publishers will generally want to see a completed fiction manuscript from a new writer. As for nonfiction works, it is possible to obtain a contract on the submission of a comprehensive outline and a couple of chapters. In this latter case, a publisher may give the author one-half of the agreed-on advance when the contract is signed and the other half when the book is completed. Some of the smaller publishers, because of limited budgets, may offer no advance but offer a contract solely on a royalty basis.

It is possible that when a completed manuscript is delivered, the publisher may declare it unsatisfactory. In such a case, the author generally has recourse to arbitration. Otherwise, any advance is the property of the author even if the book is a failure and does not sell enough copies to recoup the advance for the publisher.

For both fiction and nonfiction, reprint paperback rights are possibilities. Again to take the example of one of my students: his publisher was offered a $9,000 advance for the paperback rights to his novel. Paperback rights are divided equally between the publisher and the author, so in this case the actual amount received by the author was $4,500.

The Authors Guild in its *Guide to a Trade Book Contract* recommends a royalty of at least six percent on the first 150,000 copies sold of the paperback edition and eight percent above that amount.

You may have noted that when your newspaper in its book review supplement lists paperback best-sellers, there may be two columns, one for *trade* paperbacks and one for *mass market* paperbacks. The trade paperbacks are higher priced, use a better quality paper than the mass market paperbacks, are of various sizes and are generally sold in bookstores, while the mass market paperbacks, which conform in size for a standard 4"x7" rack slot, are found in drugstores and supermarkets in addition to bookstores.

In the event that a book is purchased by a book club, the usual division of royalties between author and publisher is 50-50. Of course, highly successful authors will be able to negotiate deals to receive larger shares of the subsidiary rights. Therefore, contractual agreements will vary from writer to writer.

If a portion of a book is serialized before trade book publication, that is, a magazine publishes a chapter or a condensed version of the book, the proceeds should go to the author, less the 10 percent commission if the author has an agent. If the author does not have an agent and the publisher should make the sale to the magazine, then the publisher may receive 10 percent of the proceeds. For motion picture rights, the proceeds will go to the author, less the agent's commission. In this case also, if the publisher should sell the motion picture rights, the publisher will receive 10 percent of the proceeds. This procedure may vary from publisher to publisher.

Most publishing contracts have an option clause, in essence giving the publisher first refusal of the author's next book. It does not mean the publisher will accept the next book. It gives the publisher the opportunity to see the new manuscript and to make a decision as to whether to publish it or not. If the publisher decides against publishing the new manuscript, the author or agent is free to go searching for other publishers.

Once a book is published, an author is usually entitled to 10 free copies. If the author wishes additional copies, they usually may be obtained at a 40 percent discount.

Payment of royalties, depending on the publisher, generally is made either quarterly or semiannually. A statement detailing the number of copies sold is included with the royalty check.

And speaking of payments, you will find that most of the major national circulation magazines which publish short stories and articles pay on acceptance. Low-budgeted magazines often pay on publication, which means that the writer is paid after his or her article is finally published. Some of the smaller magazines have a lead time of nine months. Unfortunately, there is very little you can do about the situation.

A brief note of caution: When you sell your first book, you will undoubtedly be so overwhelmed by a great wave of euphoria that you will gladly sign any contract the publisher sends you. I do reiterate that it is advisable to have the contract checked by your agent, if you have one, or by your lawyer.

TAX BENEFITS

When submitting manuscripts, writers should keep accurate records: to whom submitted, date mailed, postage paid, checks received. Also, keep your rejection slips and note on them the titles of your manuscripts; this will corroborate submissions. Keep a file of amounts spent on stationery, ititial cost of a typewriter (a one-time deduction), typewriter repairs, file cabinet or cabinets and any other items that have specifically to do with professional writing activities. Be sure you obtain receipts from the merchants for the foregoing.

The law permits professional writers certain business deductions, which can be claimed on Schedule C. Any money earned from freelance writing must be declared on your income tax return, and it, therefore, entitles you to whatever deductions the law allows.

If you own a home and set aside one room of that home for a writing studio, that room must be used solely for your writing activities. It cannot, for example, double as a bedroom. If it is used solely for writing, then you can deduct a portion of your utility bills. For example, if you live in an eight-room house, you may deduct one-eighth of the yearly home utility bills. Writers are also permitted depreciation deductions on the house on a percentage basis. I am not giving you precise percentages here because it is advisable for writers who are just joining the professional ranks to meet with an accountant to set up a business deduction schedule which can then be followed. Of course you can call an IRS office for information and guidance. But the information the IRS gives you at the time is not sacrosanct. You may find, when you send in your return, that a deduction is not allowed, and it will do you no good to argue that an IRS official gave you that guidance. You are probably better off working with experienced accountants.

There are many other deductibles to consider. If you sell a book or a story through an agent, the agent's commission is deductible. Books you buy and magazines subscribed to which are helpful in writing are deductible. If you attend a writing workshop or conference to help you in your professional writing career, the cost of the workshop or the conference is deductible. If you belong to a professional writer's organization such as the Author's Guild (you need to be a published author to belong to the Guild) the yearly dues are deductible. If you devote your time to freelance writing and have to take trips to do research for an article or a book, your auto expenses are deductible. Keep an accurate record of the travel dates and the mileage. The law allows you, currently, twenty cents a mile, which is simpler to calculate than exactly how many gallons of gas you use or how much you spend for repairs.

In your first years as a professional writer, you might show a loss on your Schedule C. This is because your expenses exceeded your writing proceeds. There is some dispute as to how much of a loss a writer can take and for how many years. The IRS can claim you are indulging in a hobby rather than a profession. You must be able to prove "an intent to make a profit."

There was a recent landmark case before the Court of Claims in which the ruling was very much in favor of the creative professional. The case was brought to the Court by a woman who was an artist in California. She had been exhibiting regularly at local galleries and had been taking business deductions. For a period of twelve years, she showed a loss each year. The IRS claimed she was not entitled to the deductions and demanded back taxes. The artist sued. The Court ruled in her favor, stating that it may take a fine artist many, many years to establish a reputation and to sell profitably, that the artist exhibited regularly at commercial galleries and was, therefore, entitled to her deductions and to claim losses.

34

As an adjunct to these deductions, it should be noted that if you are fortunate enough to write a best-seller and make a great deal of money, you can average your earnings over a period of years so that you do not suddenly face a devastating tax.

In many states, local jurisdictions will make you file a business property form and apply for a business license. As long as you file a Schedule C, you are stating that you are in business.

If you have specific questions pertaining to tax matters or other legal aspects of the writing profession, I advise you to contact a lawyer or accountant. The material in this chapter is intended only to make you aware of the complexities involved.

— Stanley Field

CHAPTER THREE

TECHNIQUES USED IN INVESTIGATIVE JOURNALISM

Finding good feature article ideas in your hometown and getting them submitted to the right editor at the right time calls for a knowledge of both research techniques and marketing. There are several tried and true systems that can be learned quickly, however.

Local interviews, home town investigative journalism, and area news coverage can be handled in several ways. Since most towns and cities contain or are near a college campus, let's begin by seeing how writers can make use of professors as interview subjects or expert sources.

PUMPING THE PROFS

My neighbor, a budding freelancer, was ecstatic recently when the editor of a local weekly newspaper told her she could do a short article on population control. She came rushing over to my house to tell about it and to ask my advice on how she should go about finding books on the subject.

"How long is this feature supposed to be?" I asked.

"Around 400 words," she said, beaming.

I pulled a hand over my face. "You're going to read a dozen books so that you can write a 400-word report?" I said. "You're crazy."

She looked perplexed. "But . . . but I need facts," she said.

I walked to a bookshelf, pulled out a small course catalog from a technical school located in our county, and a larger catalog from a university located in the city. I turned to the faculty biographies at the end of each book.

"Here," I said, pointing to several names. "These people are professors of sociology. Call them on the phone and find out which one is an expert on population control. Set up an appointment, go ask some questions, and write your article the same day."

That's just what she did . . . and is still doing at the rate of one article a week for the same editor.

Colleges are the homes of some of the greatest minds in this country, and the freelance writer who doesn't tap this source of free information is missing golden opportunities. Ideas for articles will leap out at you as you read biographical sketches of faculty members. With an idea in mind (as my neighbor had), you can call upon a professor for information.

Let's look at a typical college catalog entry and see what article ideas are waiting to be discovered:

> Louise T. Anyname, Associate Professor of Home Economics; B.S., Purdue University, 1938; M.A., Teachers College, Columbia University, 1943; Ph.D., Purdue University, 1970.

Notice that Ms. Anyname attended school during the Depression and World War II. You might find interesting stories if you asked about how she could afford college tuition during the rough Depression years or what it was like to attend college when most of the boys were away at war.

Since she earned a degree in home economics in 1938, you could ask Ms. Anyname to compare cooking, kitchen facilities, eating habits and homemaking of the 1930s to the way things are today. There might be an interesting story in why she decided after 32 years to go back for her doctorate. Along that same line, ask her to contrast her life at Purdue as a young lass of 21 with her return to Purdue as a mature woman of 52.

Other ideas could be gleaned from the same entry, but these five or six quick suggestions make it apparent that a wealth of material is there to be tapped. Be sure to explore the entire faculty gold mine. Read the college catalog for ideas, as suggested above. Read the campus newspaper for notices or small news items about instructors which you can expand for another medium.

After interviewing one professor, ask if he knows of any interesting research being done by his colleagues and then follow up on these leads. Go to the college's news bureau or public relations office and introduce yourself as a freelance writer who needs leads on professors who would make good subjects for personality profiles. Use every source.

Finally, as you are interviewing a professor, don't be afraid to emphasize that you are a *freelance* writer available to anyone for hire. If the professor makes an offhand remark like, "And I've done a lot of research in the area of genetics, but my teaching load has kept me from writing up my findings," you should immediately say that you would be happy to coauthor the article with him.

I have done this several times. When I interviewed an educational psychologist, he mentioned not having time to prepare an article on his research on child behavior. I took over his notes and later we shared a byline and a royalty check when "Assertiveness Training for Your Child" appeared in *Essence.* Similarly, with a professor of accounting I coauthored "A Plain Words Guide to Income Tax Laws" for *Essence.* I am neither a psychologist nor an accountant, but I am a trained magazine writer, and that is what these researchers needed.

Bear in mind that libraries are good information banks if you have no other place to go. But if you live near a campus, go to an expert. You will be able to focus your questions rather than spend days sifting through pages of data. You'll save time and energy, and by "pumping the profs" you might even pick up a coauthoring job or get a lead on your next article.

SMALL TOWNS AS NEWS CENTERS

Begin your search for news items by learning to listen. When you are at a PTA meeting, a church social, a garage sale or at work, close your mouth and absorb what people around you are saying. If someone is talking and others are listening, there must be something interesting being told . . . perhaps something that can be developed into a written article; so, pay attention!

38

Listen also to television and radio newscasts. Find a national news item that you can investigate locally. If the anniversary of Elvis' death is being commemorated big in Memphis, see how well his records and souvenirs are selling in your area.

Be sure to ask *enough* questions when you go out on an interview. Just because a person in your town is known for one major accomplishment, it does not mean he or she might not have done other things also worthy of writing about.

This was the case when I interviewed Ben Timmons, a champion high school wrestler who overcame a handicap of deafness to earn his place on the varsity team. After we had discussed his wrestling trophies for an hour, I asked Ben some unrelated questions about his home, parents and future plans. He told me that he had just finished an apprenticeship as a black-smith and that he was taking over a retiring man's livery stable. When I asked him how he hoped to make a living in the twentieth century with a nineteenth century skill, his answer intrigued me.

Ben explained that he had mounted an anvil, bellows, coal bed and forge onto the back of a flatbed truck and had placed a fiberglass cab over the top. He then threw in supplies of nails, horseshoes, rasps and hammers, and there he had it, a stable on wheels!

The upshot was that I wrote and sold seven articles on Ben Timmons the mobile blacksmith and nothing on Ben Timmons the deaf wrestler. As you see, finding one story can lead you to another.

I was once talking to a local man I knew through my work. He mentioned that his 65-year-old brother, Walter O. Miles, a former resident of our town, ran a printing shop in California and that for extra money he did walk-ons and bit parts in television shows and the movies. He was coming home to visit his brother; so, I set up an interview appointment.

Admittedly, Walt Miles turned out to be small pickings in the Hollywood scene, but he had been connected in minor ways with several smash movies, including a three-minutes scene in *MacArthur* and a nonspeaking role in *Close Encounters of the Third Kind.*

I could have wasted my time writing articles like, "Another Extra Tells His Story," but there would have been nothing eye-catching about such features and they would not have sold. However, I bypassed the obvious story — the tie to Hollywood — and instead focused upon the fact that when most men were getting ready to retire, Walt Miles was beginning a new and quite glamorous career.

That news peg worked very well. I sold "He Didn't Retire: He Became A Star!" to *New England Senior Citizen:* "Close Encounters of the Late in Life Kind" to the *Indianapolis Star Magazine;* "Late Blooming Hoosier Actor Faces Busy Season" to *Michiana;* "Actor Walt Miles Won't Retire" to the *Muncie Star;* "Senior Citizen Has Unique Pastime" to *Grit;* and "No Rocking Chair For Actor Walt Miles" to the *Camden Chronicle.*

Being a Hollywood extra is somewhat unusual, but being a postretirement Hollywood extra is downright unique. And, as I said before, it is being unique that makes your characters or local events "famous."

When selling one article idea to multiple markets, I use a marketing approach geared to ever-enlarging circles. I sell first to the city paper ($8-$15), next to the large statewide papers ($50-$200 for magazine supplements), then to the regional periodicals ($50-$75), go on to the national outlets ($75 and up), and whenever possible, to international publications ($50 and up).

Each time I resell the article idea, I try to make the new version different in at least three ways: (1) I provide photos of the person or event which have not appeared in other publications; (2) I insert one or two new facts about the incident which were not emphasized in a previous article; and (3) I attempt to write the article as stylistically close to the established format of the receiving publication as possible, while also trying to gear the event to its geographical locale.

For example, an area man named Pete Schlatter invented a workable two-wheel automobile one year, and I played that story for all it was worth. My first article appeared in the *Muncie Star,* a city paper, with a local-boy-makes-good-angle. It mentioned area people who had influenced Schlatter and gave a short history of his years in town. My next article appeared in the *Muncie Weekly News,* a countywide paper, with an area-resident-is-inventor angle. I next sold the article to the magazine sections of the *Indianapolis Star* and the *South Bend Tribune*, two statewide papers, with a Hoosier-man-is-unique-mechanic angle. The article covered statewide auto shows at which the car had been displayed. Afterward, I submitted the article to *Hot Rod* for national publication, focusing strictly on the auto itself, and it eventually went international when it sold to the *Christian Science Monitor* for its overseas and Canadian editions. Milking an article is a trick of the trade for a small town writer who enjoys a worldwide audience.

Once your article is written, remember to accompany it with good photos and to send it off at an advantageous time. Good photos enhance any article, particularly a personality piece. Walt Miles' agent provided me with photos of Walt and Gregory Peck in a scene from *MacArthur*.

Good timing can also generate sales. I sold the Walt Miles articles the same month that *Close Encounters* began its national television promotion. Editors love timely material, so pace your submissions.

HOMETOWN INVESTIGATIVE JOURNALISM

The investigative journalist has been gaining prestige ever since Woodward and Bernstein's *All the President's Men* came off the press in 1973. But if readers have come to appreciate the work of the investigative journalist, very few have ever learned how an investigator obtains the vast amounts of information he or she reveals in articles and books.

On the surface it seems incredible that one person could dig up so much "confidential" information. In reality, however, most investigative procedures are simple and basic. Any freelance writer could be doing the same sort of thing. The trick is, you've got to know what the procedures are. So, let's look at them.

Most freelance writers don't have an organization as powerful as the *Washington Post* available to pay them a salary while they are trying to investigate the President of the United States or members of the Supreme Court. Therefore, let's focus upon two areas in which you can earn money doing locally-based investigative articles: personality backgrounds and government operations.

Since personality backgrounds are the basis for most investigations, we'll begin there. Even if the only thing you know about a person is his or her name, there are several standard procedures you can use to dig up information on that individual.

If you know a person's name and want to find out where he or she lives, just go to your area tax collector and ask for the person's address. This is public information which must be given to any citizen upon request without charge.

Next, go to the local director of the Board of Elections. Give the director your subject's name and address and ask to see that person's voter registration. This is public information, too. The registration tells you the county and township and precinct your subject lives in, as well as the date he or she first registered to vote there and voter registration number. Most cards also have the voter's signature, which you can examine.

Then go to your county courthouse and give your subject's name and address to the county clerk and ask if there are any tax liens against him or her. It will give you some idea of the person's financial footing. Again, this is all free public information.

With the above data secured, an advisable next move is to visit your local newspaper. Explain to the supervisor of the newspaper's morgue (clipping file) that you are writing an article and that you would like to look at any available file clippings about Mr. X or Mrs. Y. Often the librarians will be glad to share whatever they have on file. These files are likely to contain job promotion announcements, civic activity interests, arrests, family births and other items which commonly appear in newspapers.

From the newspaper, your next stop is the high school your subject graduated from. Go into the school's library and ask for the yearbooks of the years your subject was in attendance. From them, make a list of your subject's school clubs, participation in sports, academic honors and positions held in student government or on the school newspaper staff. Use the library's photocopy machine to make a copy of every picture of your subject as he or she appears in the various yearbooks. Before leaving, drop by the faculty lounge and interview any teachers still on staff who knew or taught the person you are investigating.

If your subject has also attended college, send a letter to the college's Alumni Director requesting information. The Alumni Director usually will have an up-to-date address on the individual, as well as a record of employment, names of children, former addresses, major in college, parents' names and address, and any major accomplishments achieved since graduation.

Having thus gathered several pages of statistics about the subject, start interviewing the people the individual comes in contact with. Start with neighbors, business associates, friends, relatives, clients and employers or employees. Eventually you'll need to progress to the point at which you are questioning the subject's creditors for credit references and for a rundown on the subject's buying and spending habits.

Once you've mastered the procedures used in investigating individual people, you'll be anxious to try your hand at bigger game. One such challenge is to fight City Hall — or at least do a little journalistic sparring with it. Here's how to go about it.

Begin by going to your City Hall or Township Hall or County Building (or all three if you are an aggressive sort) and asking the Finance Director (sometimes called Treasurer) for a copy of the Official Budget. You may have to pay photostat costs for it, but no one can deny you your right to have a copy of it.

The Official Budget lists all revenue from local, state and federal outlets which a particular governmental unit (city, township or county) expects to receive in the coming year. It also shows where the commissioners expect to spend such incoming revenue, that is, how much for such departments as Fire, Police, Health, Sanitation and General Administration. Once the Official Budget is adopted, it can be changed only by a majority vote of the commissioners.

Having the Official Budget in hand gives you a good overview of your local government's cash flow. But it is too general to be of direct use to you. Your next move is to go to each governmental department and to request a Departmental Itemized Budget, which gives a complete breakdown of all departmental salaries and expenditures. For example, the Official Budget will reveal that $80,000 is going to be spent on the Fire Department, and the Itemized Budget will show exactly how that particular sum of money is going to be broken down. (Most governmental budgets, by the way, run concurrent with the Federal Fiscal Year of October 1 - September 30.)

With both budgets in your possession (no one can deny you access to them), you've established a data base which can help you spot potential fraud or evidence of poor governmental planning. At the end of each year get a copy of the audit of each department and compare the projected expenditures with what was actually spent. If there are any great discrepancies, you may have a potential feature story on your hands.

As with any local government report, you cannot be denied a copy of an end-of-year audit; however, it sometimes takes as much as eight weeks for audits to become available. Just leave your name and address with each departmental clerk and say, "As soon as the audit is done, please call or write to me." By law, they have to.

When you get reports, budgets and audits, you should study them carefully for "cosmetic budgeting" and "window dressing." Study small items (such as "printing costs") for hidden money. Also study "fringe benefits" for hidden money.

Here's an example of something you might discover: Under "City Retirement Fund" you see that $50,000 was budgeted. The audit shows, however, that only $30,000 was needed to cover retirement costs, and the other $20,000 was used to hire two new employees at $10,000 each. The question arises as to whether or not the inflated $50,000 budget was created purposely just so the department head could pay back political favors by hiring two of his or her friends. Check into it.

One helpful thing about audits is that they contain "footnotes" to all financial statements. These footnotes explain to the lay person exactly what is going on. They describe the total outstanding debt of the city, e.g., bonds, interest expenses and such things as any lawsuits filed against the city. You don't need to be a CPA to understand a local government audit report.

If you desire more information on each item in the Official Budget, you can have it for the price of a few stamps. The Official

Budget lists all expected local revenue, such as property taxes and assessments. *And* it lists all state and federal revenue from grants and funds.

Under state and federal revenue you'll find lump sums, such as $25,000 from HUD or $140,000 from the Department of Education. Send a letter to these state and federal departments (or phone them) and ask for a breakdown on how that money is to be spent. Usually, you will be sent both the breakdown of intended cash flow and a photostat of the actual grant which your local commissioners filed with that department.

Once you have the state and federal reports in hand, you can go to a press conference or an interview loaded for bear. Nothing is more exciting than saying something like, "Madam Mayor, in the grant you filed with HUD you told the federal government you were going to use $171,000 on low income housing this year, but the audit shows that only $150,000 was used. Why? And where is the balance of that money now?"

Or you could say, "Mr. Commissioner, in the grant you filed with the Department of Labor you said you needed $43,000 for a local CETA program to employ park workers. Why is it that now, a year later, our parks are still closed and in ill shape?"

If you start asking questions such as these, you'll not only shake up a few politicians, but also earn the quick respect of your local and regional newspaper and magazine editors. Such attention will pave the way for steady work for you as an investigative journalist.

Before we close the topic of investigations of governmental units, here are two final tips that will save you a lot of time and work:

1. The Mayor's Office can provide you with a free copy of your town or city Charter. It will explain to you every city job and the responsibilities of the person in that job.

2. If your city issues bonds, find out who the broker is and from that firm get a copy of the Prospectus. It is filled with valuable information (the quality of the city's drinking water, the miles of paved streets, etc.).

The amazing thing about investigative journalism is that it is not tremendously difficult. Nevertheless, very few freelance writers know much about it. Even many local news reporters have very limited ability when it comes to conducting a thorough investigation.

If you hone your investigative skills, you'll find that you can sell your exposés, articles and interviews to local editors, statewide Sunday supplement editors and the wire services. I am not a CPA, lawyer or private eye; still, I know what information is legally available to me and how I can obtain it. Because of this, I sell a lot of investigative articles. You can, too. It's really quite simple.

TEN TIPS ON HOW TO WORK WITH THE POLICE

TIP #1: Most police precinct houses or posts have a set time each morning at which the desk sergeant will give members of the press corps information on the previous day and night's police action (arrests, tickets, investigations). Find out the time and be on hand each day.

TIP #2: Whenever you need an official policy statement from a police post or station, get it from the highest ranking officer: sheriff, captain or post commander.

TIP #3: If there is a fatal accident on the highway, police officers have the right to withhold the name(s) of the victim(s) until next of kin are notified. However, you sometimes can get this information from a desk sergeant if you explain that your report is for an evening paper which will not come out for another six to eight hours or that you are a freelancer whose material will not appear in the local newspaper.

TIP #4: If you are doing background research on someone you have been told was arrested in his or her youth, but you cannot find any record of such an arrest at the police station, courthouse or State Records Office, don't automatically suspect fraud or a cover-up. Certain laws, such as the Holmes Youthful Offensive Act, allow reformed citizens to apply to have the records purged of any arrests which took place in their adolescence.

TIP #5: Most state police forces have a Public Affairs Bureau. Try to get on its mailing list for press releases, retirement lists, promotion lists and policy statement announcements.

TIP #6: When pressing for information, be sympathetic toward officers. Remember this important factor: if you sue under the Freedom of Information Act, the only thing they have to give you is the information you were seeking; however, if someone else sues the police for violating the Right to Privacy Act because of information you acquired and printed, the police department — and individual officers — could be liable for thousands of dollars. So, if you make your investigation seem pushy, your police contacts may feel it necessary to back away, and with good reason.

TIP #7: Many state police forces have special computer services which could be useful to you. For example, in Michigan the M.A.L.I. Program (Michigan Accident Location Index) can produce information about the number of accidents, types of accidents, existing weather conditions, citations issued, persons injured and other data for every road in every city and town in the whole state. If you earn a reputation as an honest reporter, most police post commanders will share these computer printouts with you.

TIP #8: In most states it is not very difficult to receive permission to ride for a few hours in an on-duty squad car. Go to the sheriff or other ranking officer, ask to ride in a police car and explain why such an experience would be beneficial to you. Your request will usually be accepted or denied on the spot for local police units; in state police organizations your request will be submitted to the state office and be approved or denied on that level.

TIP #9: You have the right to ask to see the police officer's report on any arrest or investigation. You are not allowed to take the report away with you or to make a photostatic copy of it; however, you may read it and make any notes about it you wish. This rule applies to all states that have either Sunshine Laws or Open Door Policy Laws.

TIP #10: If you should be denied the right to read a police report, ask the desk sergeant for a Freedom of Information form. Fill it out and turn it in. The officer will then either turn over the report to you or send it along with your Freedom of Information form to his or her superiors for a ruling. After ten days they must either give you a reply, turn the report over to you, or ask the state for an extension of (usually) 14 days. Most often you will be given access to the report or you will be sent a reply explaining why you may not see it. Sometimes reports list the names of undercover police officers or secret informants — information which may legally be withheld from you. However, whatever is in the report which is not classified must be shown to you.

TIMING AND TRENDS

Earlier in this chapter the importance of good timing in manuscript submissions was stressed. In writing for magazines timing is an especially crucial factor in gaining a sale.

In freelance magazine writing, catching trends is like bull-dogging calves: you either hit them fast or they leave you in the dust.

Freelancers have to watch for new lifestyle and writing trends with the same eagerness and attentiveness the cowboy has when waiting for a bull to rush from a rodeo pen. Here's the problem: unlike newspapers, which are put together and distributed every 24 hours, magazine issues are planned from 60 to 150 days in advance. In effect, what you are submitting in spring has to be "news" when it hits the stands in late summer or fall. And unless you are clairvoyant or are well known enough to personally *begin* a trend, you are going to need a system for predicting next season's interests.

If you develop a new style or format, a unique series idea, or some other clever writing variation, your editor will recognize it as hot stuff and will have you submit three to six additional similar articles before debuting the first one in print. By the time anyone else can steal the idea, your editor will have put out several issues featuring it. Of course, that is the same situation *you* face when you try to cash in on another writer's stylistic trend.

A better option is to catch a news trend and then beat other writers in the race to write articles about it. And you don't need psychic powers or a time machine to predict what magazine editors will be interested in publishing three to six months from now. There are some basic guidelines which, when followed, can give you the answers.

Get into the habit of reading newspaper editorials. Editors not only are very sensitive to changes in society, they are also coherent in their explanations of them and outspoken in their opinions on them.

By checking back through editorials I had clipped and saved for six months, I found four different editors who had discussed the technological benefits Americans had gained from the space program of the 1960s. This indicated a possible rising new interest in further space research programs. I immediately contacted NASA press officials and my area congressional representatives for updates on America's interest in space. It was amazing to find out there were still many projects worth pursuing. My subsequent article, "Space Pace: On the Drawing Boards, But in a Holding Pattern," was purchased by a small midwestern chain and used in nine daily newspapers.

I recommend that you clip editorials from both large and small circulation newspapers. Make sure the papers are divergent in political leanings, too. This way, if you find something being discussed by both rural and urban editors and by both Democrat and Republican sympathizers, you'll really know you've caught a universal trend. Subscribe to local newspapers and spend one day a week in the library reading out-of-state papers. Make notes of interesting commentaries and photostat any outstanding editorials you discover.

Besides tracking editorials, also monitor letters to the editor. Let's say you read the following letter in your local paper:

> I'm ticked about the way our Great American Pastime is being ignored by today's kids. I love baseball. I grew up playing sandlot ball and collecting bubblegum cards. It was great fun. Nowadays, these young whippersnappers are putting on hippie headbands and silky hotpants and are playing soccer. That's a limey sport, not American! I say we go back to developing more guys like Ted Williams and Al Kaline.

At first glance you might smile and dismiss this as the writings of some guy who needed to blow off a little steam. A closer look, however, might make you wonder if some of what he says might not be true. He might be right about the rise in popularity of soccer. And if that's a trend, you need to be checking into it.

You could phone some Little League coaches to ask if participation is down; you could contact summer playground directors and sporting goods stores to ask what is being used more, baseballs or soccer balls; and you could question youngsters in your own neighborhood about their sports preferences. You might discover that a real trend is developing in favor of soccer.

Remember that people who are set in their ways are usually the first to complain about things that alter their established lifestyles. So, by reading letters to the editor, or by listening to radio call-in shows and televised editorial rebuttals from citizens, you have good opportunities to become aware of trends and changes.

A third and less obious source of trend indicators is specialized news periodicals. Most of us receive a daily newspaper and follow television and radio news reports. These media outlets, however, only feature generalized news — that is, they focus upon items which affect the majority of people on that particular day. That's good for now, but it does you little good in predicting the news of tomorrow or next year. For that, you need to expand your reading scope.

Make it a practice to skim the tables of contents of several dozen small circulation specialty publications whenever you are in the library. Just before the natural foods fad was in full swing, an article appeared in a farming journal on how to roast acorns, and there was an article in a camping publication on six ways to make a dandelion edible. That gave me an idea. I did some more researching and eventually sold an article called "Don't Mow Your Yard — Eat It!" to a national publication. It broke in print the same month that Euell Gibbons started appearing on television to promote the "natural taste of wild hickory nuts." I had jumped in early on what soon became a very big diet trend.

A fourth place to get clues about new trends is from people involved in creative projects. When I was younger, I somehow got the crazy notion in my head that dress designers didn't want to discuss their ideas for next year's clothes, authors didn't want to discuss a work in progress and scientists didn't want to talk about their experiments until they were proved right. It turns out that that just isn't the way people really are.

Usually, the reverse is true. For example, I once called a geologist and said, "I understand that you are an authority on land revitalization. One of your colleagues told me you were spending this summer in the Arizona badlands. Are you planning on conducting any experiments there?" The geologist talked to me for an hour on the phone and later three more hours during an office appointment about a decrystalization of sand theory he had. There was no turning him off. He truly enjoyed his role as the knowledgeable authority.

I make many such phone calls each week. There are two colleges near my home; so, I keep in touch with several professors. I also phone or correspond with several politicians, writers, architects, union directors and civic leaders. The reason that many of the projects and plans these people later announce appear to be so shocking or unexpected is simply because no one ever asked them anything ahead of time. It's up to you as an investigative freelance writer to contact them, not the other way around.

In fact, that's your basic rule of thumb in the whole trend-catching process: *since people set and/or follow trends, you must keep tabs on people.* Find out what newspaper editors are telling people and what the people are responding to the editors. Find out what the specialty and creative people are writing about or developing. Get your facts written up and submitted before others get word of what's developing.

You see, unlike your friends and acquaintances who are offended by the remark, editors just love it when you can say, "I told you so."

GETTING IMPOSSIBLE-TO-GET INTERVIEWS

Another thing editors just love to hear from you is that you've landed an interview with someone who was supposedly impossible to interview. As with most tricks of the trade, landing

51

hard interviews can also be done if you know how to go about it.

I cannot begin to count the number of interviews I do each year. The personality profile sells quickly and for good money; besides, it's a fascinating specialty.

The trouble is, a lot of good writers do interviews, too. It's a wide-open market. For steady sales, you have to be the first reporter to interview a person about a new topic (which isn't as *easy* as you may think), or get interviews with people who are supposedly impossible to talk with (which isn't as *hard* as you may think).

Of the hundreds of interviews I've conducted in the last ten years, four particular ones stand out as personal achievements in my writing career. These four interviews were rated impossible to get, but I managed to get them anyway.

I interviewed then U.N. Ambassador Andrew Young after the White House put its 1978 gag order on him following his *Paris Match* interview. I interviewed Dr. Ralph Honzik, who had been the campus physician at Kent State on the day of the National Guard shootings, even though for career protection and ethical reasons he had refused to be interviewed by James A. Michener when Michener was researching his book on the Kent State ordeal.

Ed McMahon, a surprisingly jealous guardian of his privacy and a man always on the go, was also the subject of one of my interviews, as were Walter and Charlotte Baldwin (the mother- and father-in-law of the Rev. Jim Jones of Guyana), despite the fact that they had been advised by the FBI and their family attorney to talk to no one.

What gave me the edge in each case? Why was I successful where other interviewers had failed? Actually, there isn't one simple answer, but rather a combination of five different factors.

1. LUCK. Yes, there are such things as blind fate and luck, but they are no good to you unless you are ready to take advantage of them. That was the situation with Dr. Ralph Honzik.

I had met Dr. Honzik at a dinner sponsored by a social club. He had left Kent State the year after the shootings and had become a campus physician at Ball State University in Muncie, Indiana, where I was working as a reporter for the *Muncie Star.* In genuine modesty, he had kept a low profile for three years, but I just happened to catch him in a talkative mood. After identifying myself as a reporter, I asked if I could pose a few questions for a newspaper interview, and he said yes.

Since I never go anywhere without two ballpoint pens and a pocket notebook, I was able to take notes. You should get into the same habit. If possible, put a short list of basic interview questions on the back page for quick reference, too.

The questions I begin with run somewhat like this: What is a typical day like at your job? What are your short- and long-range career objectives? What are your strengths and weaknesses? What previous jobs have you held and how did you choose your current occupation? What sorts of books and magazines do you read? What are your hobbies? What part does your family play in your life? What sort of educational background do you have?

Once you've used these stock questions to get your subject relaxed and talking, you can begin to ask more direct questions designed just for that individual — for example, "How did you first learn that some of the Kent State students had been shot?"

Always be ready. You never know when you'll be seated next to a politician on a plane or find a famous actor thumbing through a book or magazine in your local bookstore. Take advantage of luck.

2. PERSISTENCE AND AVAILABILITY. The adage, if at first you don't succeed, is still valid. And it's especially true when it comes to getting interview appointments. When you are rebuffed, you must continue to call or write. Show your subject that you are serious about wanting the interview.

Furthermore, you must always make yourself available and adaptable to the subject's personal circumstances and schedule. After many rebuffs, I finally landed an interview with Ed McMahon.

I phoned the publicity director of the event at which McMahon was appearing and told her that I was a freelance writer wanting to interview Ed McMahon. She told me that she had no authority to schedule interviews and that I would have to talk to McMahon's manager or local sponsor. I had already gone that route and had been given the brush-off, so I asked her if she knew where McMahon was staying. She did and told me the name of the motel.

By waiting half a day in the lobby and then riding in the back seat of a car that was taking him to the airport, I was able to interview Ed McMahon without interrupting his schedule. Even as I was asking him questions, McMahon was eating a sandwich and studying a speech. It was awkward, but at least I got the interview and that's what counted.

The unusual circumstances of the McMahon interview also emphasize the need to be fully prepared. It's wise to use a cassette tape recorder when interviewing. (Check the batteries, microphone, and tapes to be sure everything is functioning.) Your cassettes should be 60 to 90 minutes long so that you won't have to stop your interview more than once to flip over the tape.

Some of your subjects may ask to read your interview or article before you submit it for publication. This can be both a good and a bad idea. If the person wishes only to double-check dates, figures, direct quotes and the spelling of names, such a reading can be very helpful.

However, random additional editings can sometimes ruin a manuscript's sales potential. If given a chance to edit final copy, some people will cross out references to their "graying hair" or "furrowed brow," or they will add anecdotes about their children or pets. It can be disastrous.

Each interviewer must decide whether or not to allow the subject of the interview final-draft approval. Personally, I believe I am a better judge than my subjects of how copy should be written. My practice, therefore, is to tell the subject right away that I do not give final-draft-approval privileges to my interview subjects. Some interviewers, however, consider final-draft approval a common courtesy. It's for you to decide.

To protect yourself legally from possible suits and to avoid later rebuttals, it is suggested that you do the following:

If possible, record your entire interview as evidence of what you were told.

Ask, on tape, for permission to interview your subject and record his or her affirmative response.

Explain, on tape, that you will be recording the entire interview and have your subject say, "Yes, I understand that my responses are being recorded for possible subsequent publication."

One interviewer I know goes so far as to type out an Interview Permission Form, which states that on a specified date the subject granted permission for said writer to interview him or her. Both the subject and a witness sign it. This is a rather heavy-handed option that might inhibit your subject and spoil any chance for a relaxed conversation.

You should also prepare by having plenty of questions written out — not only to help stimulate your memory, but also to over-come the inevitable dry-throat syndrome that can develop when you are suddenly face to face with a famous person.

Take notes as your subject is talking. The tape recorder preserves the conversation, but you will also need to give descriptive details with the dialogue. Since few magazines today use the straight Q & A format of transcribed dialogue, note the subject's dress style, hair, tone of voice, timbre of laugh, facial expressions and mannerisms; in short, note any physical actions that will help give the reader a visual picture of the person.

Even in a crowded room, such as at a party or a convention, your interview will be one on one. That means you have the responsibility to describe everything about the meeting. Cram as much information-gathering as you can into your limited amount of time.

3. LEVERAGE. Many times the person you are trying to interview will sidestep you, ignore your calls and refuse to acknowledge your letters. That's the time to involve a third party, a person with leverage over the person you want to interview. That could be the person's boss or sponsor or agent or public relations director or partner. Whoever it is, get to him or her and explain honestly why you feel you should have a chance to conduct the interview.

Procedures that can aid you in this process include offering the reluctant subject some guarantee, such as an advance look at some of your questions before you arrive for the interview, or some benefit, such as the good publicity the subject will gain. Your subject will not expect to be paid for sitting for the interview, and you should not offer any payment.

Should it ever mean the difference between getting an interview or not getting one, promise that you won't ask questions about sensitive topics. (For years Jerry Lewis would grant interviews only if questions about Dean Martin were not asked.) Also, point out that the interview might benefit the subject by giving him or her a chance to tell the "other side" of a controversial story.

4. SECONDARY TOPICS. Some subjects will refuse to be interviewed because they do not know what to expect. They don't know you personally, they have no idea what questions you will be asking and they may not be familiar with the publication in which the interview is to appear. To overcome these fears, stay away from your primary topic of concern and instead talk about a secondary matter, but something you know is of tremendous interest to the subject.

There is nothing fraudulent in this. After all, nothing can stop the person from suddenly starting to say, "No comment," or from showing you to the door. Most often, however, what happens is that the subject discovers that you are easy to talk to and that your only interests are listening and reporting accurately what he or she says.

In an interview with a bank president, for example, you can start off with a secondary subject, such as a hobby of rare-coin collecting, and eventually ease the person into your primary topic of what is being done to capture a team of counterfeiters who recently hoodwinked two of the bank's tellers.

That was my approach with Andrew Young. When he appeared as a guest speaker at the college I once worked for, his aide announced that no press conferences or interviews would be allowed. I approached the aide privately and asked if I could get a few quotes from the Ambassador regarding his prior visits to our campus (going back 24 years to when he came to visit one of our students, Jean Childs, whom he later married). The aide arranged for me to see the Ambassador right after breakfast the next morning. I spent more than an hour with Mr. Young and his assistant talking about many subjects. This led to a two-page spread in the *Indianapolis Star Magazine* later that month.

Parenthetically, I might add that it benefits you if you keep posted on personalities coming to area colleges, business clubs, civic theaters, and the like. In order to get good interviews, you have to be aware of where the best prospects for interviews are going to be.

5. NONPROFESSIONAL CONTACTS. Sometimes interviews can be set up only after you approach several people who can lead you to friends or relatives of your target subject. At times, a whole chain of people is involved. For example, if you have a friend who has a brother who has a roommate who has a cousin who once dated Eddie Murphy, having successive meetings with these people may be your only way of getting to interview Murphy himself.

Unlike sponsors or managers, these people have no leverage over the person you want to interview. They cannot schedule or order an interview. But they can at least put you in touch with your subject.

In this chapter we learned several tricks of the writing trade. We learned that professors at colleges can be good sources for information and story ideas. We learned that even a small town can be brimming with leads for feature stories. We learned how to predict and write about trends. We learned how to get interviews even when they are supposed to be impossible to get. In the next chapter, we will look at several other lucrative avenues for freelancers.

— Dennis E. Hensley

CHAPTER FOUR

THE FREELANCE CORRESPONDENT

In chapter three you were shown how journalists do investigative digging in order to find answers to questions relating to police and governmental matters and article research. There are other areas of journalism which freelance writers also can be involved in: regional correspondence; column writing; book reviewing; and interviewing. In this chapter we will take a look at these other four areas.

REGIONAL CORRESPONDENCE

One of the best ways for a beginning freelance writer to gain experience, obtain regular bylines and earn some money is to become a regional correspondent for a newspaper or magazine.

The regional correspondent (or "stringer") covers news which occurs in a specific area — one city, one county or perhaps one state — and reports that news on a regular basis to the home office of the publication for which he or she works. For example, during four years in which I lived in the small town of North Manchester, Indiana, I worked as a regional correspondent for the Fort Wayne *News-Sentinel.* If anything newsworthy occurred in my town or county, I would look into it and either phone or mail in a story to the Fort Wayne newspaper, forty-five miles away.

Since it is virtually impossible for major statewide newspapers to cover all newsworthy events in each of the towns they circulate to, the newspapers are eager to find qualified correspondents to assist in this process. The correspondents usually file brief reports on local election results, new local laws, school board meetings, major automobile accidents, intriguing local crimes, important business developments and such annual events as festivals, parades, high school sports playoffs and church socials. Additionally, correspondents occasionally contribute journalistic profiles of local civic, business and religious leaders.

Sample Letter To Use When
Applying to Be a Regional Correspondent

May 10, 1984

Sam D. Writer
777 Seventh Street
Localville, Michigan 48706

Louise R. McBridge
Managing Editor
The Detroit Tribune
333 Coldwater Avenue
Detroit, Michigan 49901

Dear Louise R. McBridge:

I am interested in becoming a regional correspondent for *The Detroit Tribune*. I live in Localville and have both the time and the accessibility to cover news throughout Davis and Casselwood counties.

I am 26 years old and I am one of three partners who own and operate a small print shop in Localville. Since I can work at hours of my own choosing, I am free to set my own schedule. This would make me available to cover any newsworthy event that might occur in my area.

During high school I was sports editor of our high school newspaper for two years. I graduated from Huron Junior College with a two-year Associates degree in English in 1980. I've sold 18 freelance articles to small circulation magazines during the past three years. I've always enjoyed writing and I know I could do a good job for you.

Enclosed are two articles which I prepared for your possible use in getting me started. One is a short interview with Mrs. Marie White, our town's first female firefighter; the other is a summary of last night's school board meeting. I also own a 35mm camera in case photo coverage would be needed for future assignments.

I will enjoy hearing from you on this matter at your convenience. My telephone number is (517) 555-8362. Thank you for your time.

Respectfully yours,

Sam D. Writer

To become a regional correspondent, prepare a letter to send to the managing editor of a newspaper which is sold in your town yet is located some distance away. In the letter explain that you wish to become a regional correspondent for that newspaper. Mention your credentials and experience. Include several sample articles which have current news value. If you have written for other publications previously, you may also wish to send along copies of two or three of your printed articles.

Once accepted as a correspondent, you will be given a press card, which will give you access to meetings and social events in which members of the press corps have privileged treatment. Although you will carry a press card, you will still technically be a "freelance" writer. The newspaper will not put you on salary; instead, you will be paid according to the number of published articles and news items you turn in. You will not be given any of the benefits which full-time staff reporters receive (retirement plans, workman's compensation, paid vacations, etc.); however, you will also not have to work set hours the way full-time reporters must.

The best benefit you receive as a regional correspondent is the opportunity to cover a story for a newspaper but not have to sell all rights to your story to that newspaper. This enables you to later resell your articles to other periodicals. And that's a real benefit. Let me explain.

A full-time reporter who works for a newspaper or magazine as a salaried employee is said to be doing "work made for hire." This means that his or her employer *owns* all rights to the articles that reporter prepares for that periodical. You, however, are not on salary. Once your freelance article appears in the newspaper you work for as a regional correspondent, that article then can be sold elsewhere by you.

Here's an example of how it works. Let's say that a famous television star has been hired to come to your city to help publicize the opening of a new bank. While in town, this famous person grants you an interview. Naturally, you will quickly write, then call in, your interview to the newspaper you work for as a regional correspondent. The next day your article will be printed in that newspaper. After that, you are free to reclaim possession of your article (as well as your notes, taped interview and photographs of the celebrity) and begin to sell the same article, or

A Sample Model's Release

In consideration for value received, receipt whereof is acknowledged, I hereby give (name of freelance photographer) the absolute right and permission to copyright and/or publish, and/or resell photographic portraits or pictures of me, or in which I may be included in whole or in part, for art, advertising, trade or any other lawful purpose whatsoever.

I hereby waive any right that I may have to inspect and/or approve the finished product or the advertising copy that may be used in connection therewith, or the use to which it may be applied.

I hereby release, discharge and agree to save (the accepting publication) from any liability by virtue of any blurring, distortion, alteration, optical illusion or use in composite form, whether intentional or otherwise, that may occur or be produced in the making of said pictures, or in any processing tending toward the completion of the finished product.

Date _____ Model _____

Address _____

_____

Witness _____

variations of it, to other magazines and newspapers. In this way, you may wind up making six or eight article sales, whereas the salaried reporter is limited to just the one sale to his or her employer publication.

As you can quickly figure out, being a regional correspondent will not only keep you busy for one periodical, it will also provide many opportunities for you to do spinoff marketing of your articles and features. It is an excellent way for the beginning freelance writer to get involved in the publishing process.

Tips For Photo-Journalists

#1 Don't be afraid to move, direct, and impose upon your subjects in order to set up the type of picture you want to take.

#2 Shoot plenty of photos, but change the settings so that your photo essay does not seem redundant (different views, different rooms, different people).

#3 Whenever possible, avoid artificial lighting. Try to make your photos seem real, not stiff or posed or unnatural.

#4 Take a picture of anything that strikes you as interesting; make both a horizontal and a vertical shot of it if time and film permit.

#5 Only include mood shots or experimental photography (blurred images, fish-eye lenses) after you have sent an editor plenty of straight standard journalistic photos.

#6 Have a rubber stamp made with your name and address on it and a mention of the rights you are selling to your photographs. Stamp this information of the back of each of the photos you submit to an editor.

#7 When mailing photos, place them between two pieces of sturdy cardboard and send them in an envelope which you have clearly marked "PHOTOGRAPHS: Do Not Bend."

#8 Make the setting of your photos appropriate to the person you are writing your article about (shoot a tennis pro on the courts, shoot a business executive in a business office, shoot a gas station attendant with his station in the background).

#9 Get yourself a paraphernalia bag to carry along on assignments. Inside it, put your notepads, extra rolls of film, pencils and pens, spare lenses, and other needed items of equipment or extras.

#10 When in doubt, use a model release form for subjects you feel may later regret they posed for photos. Always use a model release form when putting someone into a photograph that will be used to endorse something or someone.

#11 When writing captions for your photos, provide all the necessary information. Your caption should identify everyone in the picture, tell when it was taken, where it was taken, and have all people and place names spelled correctly.

#12 Keep your negatives. Start a subject/index file so that you can get at the photos you need without any delay or trouble.

#13 Be familiar with the Copyright Laws as they apply to photographs.

#14 Move closer, not farther away, on most shots. Pictures taken from far away show too much background and clutter.

#15 If your shutter speed is shorter than 1/125th of a second, use a tripod.

COLUMN WRITING

Another good way to break into freelance journalism is to come up with a good idea for a column and then find a newspaper which will run your columns on a regular basis. Most readers are familiar with the well-known columnists such as William Buckley, Carl Rowan, Erma Bombeck, Ann Landers and Sylvia Porter who specialize in one particular area (politics, black issues, comedy, advice or finances). These columnists have high visibility because their columns are syndicated through a wire service and, thus, are published daily in hundreds of newspapers.

What is more important for you to realize, however, is that there are thousands of other columnists who are also being published on a regular basis, even though to a much smaller readership. All newspapers are on the lookout for writers who can come up with an entertaining or informative topic for a column which can be sustained for a long time.

When I first became interested in active freelance writing, I approached the editor of the *Muncie Star* with the idea of letting me write a column about country music. I submitted five sample columns. After reading the columns, the editor agreed to give the column a chance. Under the name "Country News and Views," my columns ran one at a time for five consecutive Saturdays. Response from the readers was so positive, I was allowed to continue the column on Saturdays for the next two years. Later, I also began a column for the Sunday edition which I called "Dust Jacket Reviews" in which I profiled authors and reviewed new books.

Sit down for a moment and make a list of subjects you really feel you know a great deal about. Columns now appearing in local newspapers cover such topics as dog grooming, travel, cooking, gardening, retirement, crafts, hobbies, investments, real estate, medicine, hunting, home decorating, sewing, sports, the arts, politics and marriage counselling. No doubt your list will contain equal or greater varieties of subjects.

From your list, focus on the topic you know best and enjoy discussing most. Take five aspects of this topic and prepare one column (approximately 300-600 words) on each aspect. Submit these five columns to your local newspaper along with a cover letter explaining your writing experience *and* your experience related to the subject of your column.

Allow the editor a week to respond to you. If you do not receive a letter or phone call, you then may wish to call the editor or visit his office to see if there was any interest in your column idea. If not, don't be discouraged. Just submit your sample columns to another newspaper, and then another, until you find an editor who is interested in your column.

Although writing a column for a local newspaper may not pay as well as you would like it to (usually from $5 to $40 per column), it will provide several additional benefits. You will get a lot of writing experience and a lot of exposure for your byline; you will become well-known as an expert in a certain field and this will open doors for you when you want to write freelance articles to national magazines which specialize in that field; and you will begin to amass a series of informative clippings which you later may be able to develop into a book.

If your column is very successful in your local paper, you later can take samples of it and submit them to the various wire services. If your writing style has reader appeal and your column has broad reader interest, you may one day find yourself among the ranks of the nationally syndicated columnists.

BOOK REVIEWING

Many very famous writers — Edgar Allan Poe, W. Somerset Maugham, John Updike, to name just three — used book reviewing as a way of both beginning and maintaining a professional reputation as competent critics and writers. Book reviewing is one of the easiest ways for a beginning writer to gain journalistic experience and byline exposure.

Most newspapers do not pay much for book reviews (you do, however, get to keep the books you review). Still, most writers are avid readers and book reviewing enables them to gain something tangible from all that time spent reading.

There is a five step process for landing a job as a reviewer. First, set up an appointment to meet the arts editor of your local newspaper. Second, present credits, reading habits and memberships in literary clubs. Third, give the editor a typed copy of a 375-word review of a newly released book and tell the editor you would appreciate it if he or she would read it at his or her convenience. Tell the editor that you are offering the review for publication. Fourth, go home, read another book, write another review and contact another editor. Fifth, continue this practice until an editor somewhere accepts your review. As soon as you see your review in print, send the editor two more reviews.

Whenever possible, review a new book by an author you already know well from previous reading so that you can bring some additional experience to your review. Make notes on your book's margins or on a notepad as you are reading; don't trust your memory for all the details. If possible, wait for at least one day after you've read the book before you write your review; without consulting your notes at first, see which parts of the book are still vivid in your mind and then use these as a basis for your review.

Each book review must list the basic data about the book: its title, author, publisher and price. The review should discuss the major protagonists (heroes) and antagonists (villains) and explain why they are key persons in the plot. The review should also provide a basic plot summary, but one which does not give away the ending. The reviewer should relate his impressions and opinions of the book. Also, it should be mentioned if there is anything special about that particular book; it may be a reissue of an old book or a sequel to an earlier book or perhaps one book in a long series of books on one topic.

When writing your review, be informative but not concerned with trivial details. Write in a readable style and don't be too dependent on similes and metaphors. If you have negative things to say about a book, do so in as constructive a way as possible. Don't be influenced by other reviewers or by publishers' publicity sheets.

Being a book reviewer will often make you a better critic of your own writing. It will expose you to a variety of writers and writing styles, it will increase your home library, it will help you get into print and it will help expand your reputation as a writer and critic.

INTERVIEWING

In previous decades, journalism was considered a fact-finding profession. Reporters were expected to present the who, what, when, where, why and how aspects of a story in as straightforward a manner as possible. Today, with the advent of radio talk shows and television news magazines, journalism has added such words as *personality, style, impact, trend* and *reaction* to its original five Ws and an H.

Nowhere are such changes more evident than in the journalistic interview (or "personality profile"). Readers today want more than simple statistics about people: they want to know what motivates them to do and say the things they do.

To capture this extra quality in an interview, the freelance writer has to know what factors lead to a successful interview experience. Surprisingly enough, the preparation which leads up to the interview is usually far more taxing, and certainly more involved, than the actual interview itself. Let's review some of the basics of journalistic interviewing.

Prior to the interview you should do extensive research on your subject. Begin to put together a dossier on the individual. Find copies of whatever has already been written about the subject and read each article carefully. Ask other people about their relationships with this person. Study whatever he or she is famous for (paintings or books or movies, etc.). Whenever possible, conduct the interview on the subject's home turf (office or home or job location).

Prepare a list of questions and arrange them on notecards in logical order. Include several open-ended questions which cannot be answered with a simple "yes" or "no." Ask one question at a time; no five-parters, please. Hold your roughest questions until last.

Tape-record your conversation. If your subject is intimidated by a recorder, say that you will turn it off whenever an off-the-record statement is to be made. (After a few minutes, the subject usually forgets about the recorder anyway.) If the subject refuses to allow a tape recorder to be used, you must then resort to notes; but be sure to verify quotes by saying, "Now let me see if I have

Necessary Information About an Interview Subject

Full Legal Name
Date of Birth
Place of Birth
Father's Occupation
Mother's Occupation
Siblings' Names and
 Birth Dates
Famous or Important
 Relatives
Family Pets
Father's Philosophy of
 Life/Work
Mother's Philosophy of
 Life/Work
Lesson Learned from
 Parents
Childhood Friends and
 Neighbors
Childhood Escapades,
 Hobbies, Accidents
Grade School Name,
 Location and Years
 Attended
 A. Favorite Teachers
 B. Favorite Subjects
 C. Noteworthy
  Incidents
High School Name,
 Location, and Years
 Attended
 A. Type of Classes
 B. Sports
 C. Scholastic Honors
 D. Extracurricular
  Activities
College Names, Locations and Years Attended
 A. Degrees
 B. Sports and Extracurricular Activities
 C. Scholarships, Grants, Honors, Awards
 D. Part-time and/or Summer Jobs
Military Background
Family Background

Height
Weight
Color of Eyes
Color of Hair
General Health
Gestures, Mannerisms
Tone of Voice
Facial Expressions
Manner of Dress
Size and Appearance
Demeanor
Office Surroundings
Job Title, Responsibilities
Personal Triumphs,
 Failures
Achievements
Pet Peeves
Career Turning Points
Daily Routine
Leisure Activities
Clubs, Civic Groups
Avocations
Reading Preferences
Arts Enjoyed
Future Plans
Things You Wish You Had
 Done Differently
Philosophy of Life/Work
World Travels
Religious Beliefs
Political Leanings

Sample Open-End Questions

1. What, in the last year, has given you the most pleasure?

2. What do you like and dislike most about yourself?

3. Who are your heroes . . . living or dead?

4. Which have you enjoyed more, getting to the top or being on top? Why?

5. What do you envision yourself doing in ten years?

6. For what act or achievement would you most like to be remembered?

7. Is there anything you haven't accomplished that you would like to?

8. Who makes you laugh?

9. If you were hospitalized for three months but were not really too sick, whom, and it can't be a relative, would you want in the next bed?

10. What are your favorite books?

11. Describe for me your idea of a perfect day.

12. If you were not doing the work you are now doing, what would you most likely be doing?

13. If you could be any person in history, whom would you choose?

14. Who was the first girl/boy you were ever in love with?

15. If you were suddenly given a great deal of money and told to spend it on yourself, what would be the first thing you'd buy?

16. What is your favorite fantasy?

this correct. You said . . . ." Ask your subject to spell names of people, companies and places he or she mentions which are unfamiliar to you.

Show genuine interest, but be nonemotional. If a subject happens to mention that he shot his wife and buried her in the backyard, stay calm and keep the interview moving along. If you look startled, he will say, "Oh, that's off the record," and your interview will die right along with the guy's wife.

Accuracy is extremely vital. Don't misquote a person unless you are prepared for a lawsuit.

Never destroy or erase your tapes. They are your proof that you heard what was said. Make more than one appointment to interview your subject if his or her schedule is rigid. Get all the material you can and then sift out the best information and quotes.

EFFECTIVE LISTENING

One of the best ways to become an effective interviewer is to learn first how to be an effective listener. A truly effective listener has the ability to take mental notes, to use good body language and to keep his or her mind from wandering from the topic at hand. Let's review some basic ways in which you can work to become a better listener.

First, remember to maintain eye contact with the person who is speaking to you. If your eyes are focused on the other person's eyes, instead of staring off into space or glancing down at some notes in your hands, the speaker will know that he or she has your undivided attention. This will give the speaker a feeling that you are taking seriously what is being said.

Second, use body language that emphasizes that you are paying attention. Sit near the person, not across the room. Lean slightly forward, as though you truly desire to hear every word being spoken. Occasionally nod your head affirmatively to non-orally announce agreement with or understanding of what is being said.

Third, listen closely to what is being said and keep your mind on the topic at hand. Don't let your mind wander. Don't try to anticipate what the speaker is going to say next, and don't spend a lot of time trying to make up clever responses. If you are really paying attention, you'll grasp the complete story of what the other person is saying. In doing this, your responses will later come very naturally.

Fourth, use short lulls in the conversation and moments of silence to add weight to your discussions. Selling bottle openers or magazines door to door may call for a fast-talking salesperson; maintaining a good interview rapport, however, is accomplished when you take the time to think carefully about what the other person has said before you react to it. By taking a moment before responding to the interview subject's conversation, you give the impression that your mind has been completely occupied with what he or she has been saying; now, you are taking a moment to reflect on it and to formulate a proper response. This gives credibility to your reputation of being a good listener.

Fifth, remember to observe common courtesy. Don't cut someone off in the middle of a sentence and don't stifle conversations by injecting snide or negative remarks. Don't talk along with people, anticipating their words and echoing them; if you have this nervous habit, start controlling it. Don't put words into people's mouths: let them explain things in their own ways.

SUMMARY

Freelance writers often can get started as working writers by becoming involved in some phase of journalism. Since there are tens of thousands of newspapers in America, the opportunities are limitless for the freelance writer to find an opening as a correspondent, columnist, reviewer or interviewer. Freelance journalism offers a variety of ways to gain experience, accumulate byline credits and earn some money, too.

— Dennis E. Hensley

CHAPTER FIVE

FEATURE WRITING

Magazines, newspapers, Sunday supplements and quarterly journals eagerly seek a variety of feature stories for each of their issues. The feature article has been a mainstay for the freelance writer for many years. In this chapter we will look at how to find feature story ideas, how to market them to the correct magazines, and how to write them in a salable manner.

WHAT TO WRITE ABOUT

In order to sell magazines, editors have to offer articles which readers will be anxious to read. There are certain subjects which are recurring favorites with readers, and if you are aware of them, you will find ready markets for your material.

(1) *Money.* Readers are fascinated by articles which explain new ways to save, spend, make, collect and use money. If you have an innovative approach to establishing an IRA or saving grocery coupons or reducing taxes, you'll find a market for your article.

(2) *Physical Fitness.* Editors are constantly looking for articles on new diets, innovative exercise programs, ways to live longer and tips for looking better.

(3) *How-to Features.* Readers frequently buy magazines because they contain articles which teach such things as how to fix a chair, buy a car, apply for a job or plan a vacation. The standard "how-to" article is always a popular feature. If you know how to teach people how to do something in a faster, cheaper or better way, get it down on paper and send it to an editor.

(4) *Mental Health.* Today's society is being confronted by a multitude of problems such as unemployment, inflation, computerization, population control, family disintegration and race relations. This has led to mental and emotional problems in many people. Editors are seeking articles on such topics as

overcoming stress, handling burnout and dealing with personal acceptance problems. Interviews with psychologists and psychiatrists on these and related topics will find ready markets.

(5) *Lifestyles.* People are intrigued by the way other people live and work and socialize. How does a monk exist in solitude? Why does a millionaire continue to maintain a 60-hour work week? What does a king eat for breakfast? These and similar questions are answered in lifestyle features about both common and uncommon people. Editors are always on the lookout for captivating features about people with unusual lifestyles.

(6) *Profiles.* Along with lifestyles, readers also like to know about people themselves, particularly famous or unusual people. In my years as a journalist I've had a chance to interview many celebrities, from Dolly Parton to former U.N. Ambassador Andrew Young. Naturally, features on such people are easy to sell. But equally easy to sell are articles on unusual people. I've already mentioned the boy who became a blacksmith with a mobilized livery stable and the retiree who became a movie actor at age 68. I've also sold articles on a man who invented a two-wheel car, a man who collected 54,000 specimens of moths, a woman who created quilt designs, and more. Their unusual stories and unique personalities made very readable copy.

(7) *Activities.* With the advent of many of our modern time-saving devices, many people are finding themselves with time on their hands. They often turn to magazines for ideas on ways to fill their time. They are seeking ideas for individual activities (crafts, projects), family activities (games, outings, celebrations) or group activities (parties, trips, programs, seminars, workshops). If you have ideas and answers, you'll find editors eager to see them.

(8) *Self-Help Ideas.* Readers are always on the lookout for feature articles which can show them ways to advance themselves. Articles on how to dress for success, improve one's grammar, enhance one's public image or help develop a more positive outlook on life are always of interest to editors.

(9) *Amusement.* People frequently discover interesting places to visit, things to see and people to watch by reading feature articles about these topics in magazines. If you have an idea for an entertainment-related feature, no doubt you will find a market

How to Analyze a Magazine

If there is a particular professional journal or trade magazine which you would like to write for, you will need to know how to provide what that publication is looking for. Here is a five-step process you can use to analyze a magazine.

1. SLANT — No magazine is completely devoid of a "view" of the way things should be. The more specialized the magazine, the narrower the viewpoint. So, read the magazine to discover what its views are on business, family life, patriotism, religion and everything else. If your material can match the magazine's view of things, you'll increase your chances of getting published.

2. METHODS OF COMMUNICATION — Each magazine will use specific ways of getting its information across to the readers. Some use long articles; some use photos, maps and charts; some use cartoons. Examine the magazine carefully and then submit material in a format which will best match the magazine's format.

3. VARIETY — Check the magazine to see how many different topics it covers each issue. Are they varied or related to one primary topic? Also, check to see how many different styles of writing the magazine uses — fiction? nonfiction? humor? interviews?

4. BALANCE — Decide how much of the magazine is devoted to each major topic of interest it focuses upon. For example, if it is an insurance magazine and 30 percent of its articles and ads relate to ways to canvass cold calls, your article on that subject would have three chances in ten of getting published.

5. COMPREHENSIVENESS — How in-depth are the reporting and writing in the magazine you are examining? Does it offer a passing reference to the subject you are interested in, or does it analyze every minute detail of that subject? You will have to adjust your articles to correspond in depth and research to whatever the magazine usually publishes.

for it. Make it newsy, fill it with specifics related to costs, dates and reservations and give a general overview of the entertainment aspects of the topic.

(10) *Schooling Innovations.* Parents, students, teachers, seminar leaders and a host of other people with a connection to teaching are interested in reading about new ways to educate students (of all ages). If you can write about using the computer in the classroom or learning subconsciously while sleeping or making the "open-room" concept more effective, you will have editors eager to see your manuscripts. Anything new and exciting about the educational process is of interest to editors and readers.

BRAINSTORMING A FEATURE ARTICLE

Prior to writing a feature article, it is best to sit down and carefully think about what you want the feature to accomplish. The two most important things you'll need to decide are *who are your intended readers* (children? adults? professional people? laymen?) and *what is the purpose of the feature* (to entertain? to report on something? to teach?). Once you are sure about these two items, you will have a better understanding of what your article's format, tone, style, vocabulary level and length should be.

As you begin to write your feature, remember to tell things in a logical order so that time sequences and occurrences of events are related to the reader in a smooth and fluid way. Too many flashbacks can be annoying to readers. Also, use smooth transitions which will help the reader ease from one topic to the next. (More on this later in the chapter.)

In writing the feature, remember that your job is not to impress people with your sophisticated syntax or your large vocabulary; your job is to communicate. As such, write with short, familiar words and usually in sentences of fewer than fifteen words. Keep your paragraphs short, for eye appeal. Vary your sentence lengths and patterns; don't have every sentence follow a subject-verb-object format.

Avoid street jargon, cliches, generalities and malicious statements. Use specific words and phrases. For example, you should use picture nouns and action verbs. The noun *house* is a generality, but the nouns *mansion* and *shack* are specific words that put a picture in your reader's mind. Similarly, the verb *hit* is rather ambiguous, whereas the verbs *slap* or *tap* pinpoint the precise action which took place.

Put words you want to emphasize at either the very beginning or the very end of your sentence. If you wish to stress a time element, for example, you can say, "Now is the time for every good man to come to the aid of his country" or "It is the time for every good man to come to the aid of his country now." Notice how the word *now* (and its emphasis) gets lost when you say, "It is the time now for every good man to come to the aid of his country."

Generally, it is more effective for you to write your features in the active voice. It makes the copy seem closer to the action and it cuts out many unneeded words. For example, in the passive voice you would write, "The book was given to Tom by Bill." That sentence has a "distance" from what happened; it is also eight words long. In the active voice the same sentence would be, "Tom gave Bill the book." This sentence seems to bring the reader closer to the action; and it only requires five words.

In your features, don't try to imitate someone else's writing style. Be yourself. The short choppy sentences of Hemingway, the long flowing sentences of Faulkner, the precise syntactical balance of James and the yarn-spinning ramblings of Twain are unique to their authors. You be unique, too. You cannot become successful by trying to create cloned articles or stories in someone else's style.

BLUEPRINT FOR FEATURES

One of the hardest problems which beginning feature writers have to face is how to organize a feature. To help alleviate this problem, let me provide you with an outline of what a feature article should contain and how it should be structured.

Outline for Preparing Features

I. Brainstorm and Plan
   A. Select an Interesting Topic
      1. Make up a working title for the feature
      2. Determine the audience
      3. Define the purpose of the feature
      4. Check to see what has already been written on that topic
      5. Make a list of potential markets for the feature
   B. Initiate the Research
      1. Make notes from books and magazines
      2. Interview experts on this subject
      3. List your own experiences in this area
      4. Order pertinent pamphlets, brochures or reprints
      5. Attend classes or seminars on the topic

II. Prepare the Rough Draft
   A. Organize Your Data
      1. Select one specific aspect of the subject
      2. Arrange pertinent data in a logical sequence
      3. Outline a format for the feature
   B. Write the First Draft
      1. Prepare a lead with a solid reader hook
      2. Use topic sentences to introduce new ideas
      3. Use summary sentences to conclude explanations
      4. Use good transitions between paragraphs
      5. Keep the writing simple, direct, readable and obvious
      6. Use picture nouns and action verbs
      7. Vary the sentence lengths

III. Write the Final Draft
   A. Edit Your Rough Draft
      1. Check for spelling, grammar or punctuation errors
      2. Eliminate cliches, street jargon, or misused words
      3. Make sure all explanations are simple and obvious
      4. Double-check statistics, dates, addresses and titles
   B. Evaluate the Writing Style
      1. Read the feature aloud to check rhythm, word choice and pace
      2. Make sure the article ends with something that teaches or amuses the reader

IV. Type the Final Draft
   A. Use Proper Materials
      1. White bond paper of #16 or #20 weight
      2. Dark typewriter ribbon
   B. Follow Standard Format
      1. Use 1¼" margins on each page
      2. Double-space all typing
      3. Type on one side only
      4. Put name and address in upper left corner of first page
      5. Put "rights" offered and word count in upper right corner of first page
      6. Center title on page, 15 spaces down from the top
      7. Put byline centered under title
      8. Begin manuscript on first page
      9. Type the word "more" at the bottom of each page which leads to another

V. Mail the Manuscript
   A. Add a cover letter to your manuscript
   B. Paperclip (never staple) your pages together
   C. Enclose a self-addressed stamped envelope
   D. Insert a piece of cardboard to keep the envelope flat
   E. Provide special cardboard protection for any photographs which may accompany the feature

USING TRANSITIONS

In making the various parts of your outline flow together well, you will need to know how to create smooth transitions. The various parts of the outline don't just automatically blend, they must be helped.

Have you ever read an article or story which seemed to have its paragraphs stacked atop each other like airplanes over LaGuardia at midday? Boring, isn't it?

Actually, it's worse than boring. It's confusing and tedious, and certainly unprofessional.

The problem is a lack of good transitions. The author has not helped you get from one topic to the next. Instead, he or she has simply spliced together a series of ideas. It doesn't work.

Sample Title Page

Legal Name Here   Rights Offered Noted Here
Address Here   Fiction/Nonfiction Noted Here
City, State, Zip Code   Word Count Here

Your Title Goes Here

By Your Name

The manuscript should be typed double-spaced. There should be one-and-a-quarter inch margins on all sides. Even block quotes and footnotes should be double-spaced. The title of your article should not be put in all capital letters. If you use a pen name, your legal name should be typed in the upper left hand corner (so that the payment check can be made out to and mailed to the right person) but your pseudonym should be listed as the byline under your title.

At the top of page two and all following pages, type your last name and one key word from the title (in quotation marks) and the page number. For example: Hensley, "France," p. 8. When typing, use a dark ribbon and make sure that your keys are clean. Type on just one side of the page. Make accent marks and other diacritical marks in ink after you have finished typing. Proofread your manuscript carefully before mailing it.

(more)

Just as a train can't hold its cars together and run smoothly without couplers, an article or story cannot link its paragraphs together and proceed smoothly without transitions. Transitions help the reader to advance from one subject to the next in a natural sequence. They lead the reader to believe that the article or story is proceeding in the only direction it could possibly go.

But trying to create a natural transition is not always easy. We can all recognize stilted transitions, such as those used in low budget movies ("Meanwhile, back at headquarters . . . ."). They stand out like neon signs. They interrupt the flow of an article rather than enhance it. Transitions should be subtle; they should ease the reader along in one direction, not "kick" him or her along.

Many feature articles, by necessity, call for changes in setting, time, action and sometimes even subjects. Without smooth transitions, these changes become jolts — and readers hate jolts.

Whether you know it or not, you are already somewhat of a master of transistions. In everyday conversation you constantly use oral transitions like these: "Speaking of funny incidents, that reminds me . . ." "If you think that's something, you should hear what Shirley did last week . . ." or "Hey, let me tell you my side of it . . . ."

These spoken transitions shift the topic of conversation without completely breaking the original train of thought. They prepare or "set up" the listener for the story about to be shared. Your written transitions should function in a similar manner. Let's review some of the basic methods of developing transitions.

(1) *Comparison and Contrast.* The easiest way to move from one subject to the next is to compare or contrast the two. For example, if you're moving from a focus on one brother to another brother, you could say, "Since Bob wanted to be just like his brother Bill, he always wore white sneakers, chewed gum and combed his hair straight back, too." This compares the two brothers.

Equally effective would be to contrast the two brothers, with a sentence such as, "Whereas Bill was fair-haired and tall like his father, Bob had the olive skin and raven hair of his mother." A third option would be both to compare *and* contrast the brothers: "Like Bill, young Bobby liked fast cars; but whereas Bill's dreams ended at being a driver, Bobby had ambitions to own the entire speedway one day."

(2) *Turning-Point Questions.* A frequently-used method of arriving at the answer to a problem raised in an article is the technique of stating the problem as a question. One then can proceed to a detailed response.

For example, if you were writing an article about U.S. and Mexican political relations, you might use this transition format:

Mexico has no nuclear weapons, no standing army of any great merit, no submarines, no aircraft carriers and no major radar installations. Why then is the U.S. Secretary of State working 24 hours a day to secure Mexico as a military ally?

The answer is simple. Oil.

Mexico has it and we need it.

A turning-point question focuses the reader's attention on a specific single problem. The only natural thing that could follow would be an answer to that problem. Thus, you are able to make the transition from background material to new information without jolting the reader during the shift.

(3) *Raised Expectations.* One way to move a reader from one paragraph to the next is to suggest that all is not well with your characters or plot. Your reader will then continue to read ahead in expectation of an explanation of the tension. Here's an example of a raised expectation transition:

As the stranger continued to talk in his casual manner, the sentry made the mistake of assuming the man meant him no harm. He carelessly lowered his rifle.

Although we don't know yet what will happen between the stranger and the sentry, we are prepared for some kind of action to take place. When it does (in the next paragraph), it seems logical to us. The transition prepared us for it.

(4) *Correlations.* When you need to provide background information or a flashback scene for your reader but don't want to jar the flow of your article or story, you can have your main character see something or pick up something and then correlate that object to the background information. It works this way:

Tom rubbed the apple against his sleeve. Funny thing about apples. Most people associated them with Adam and Eve or William Tell or Isaac Newton. But not Tom. Every time he held an apple, he thought of Grampa Ross.

The human senses are constantly sending data to the brain. Since they cause the brain to think of myriad different things, readers will identify with (and accept) the use of an object as a stimulant for generating tangent thoughts. By correlating an object to some relevant flashback information, you can ease the reader from the present to the past in your writing.

(5) *Summarization.* Readers grow weary of repetitious detail in writing. They prefer to have the feature progress rapidly. To accomplish this, you sometimes will have to write transitions which provide brief summaries of background material. Such summaries can quickly get you to the crux of the next action scene. Note this example:

> Mike could feel perspiration forming on his lip and forehead. The first six innings of the game had been simple. His curve had broken perfectly and his fast ball had left Deckerville's batters blinking. But now it was different. Between innings his shoulder muscle had flared up again.

Here we have summarized the action of the first six innings, and thus have carefully transposed the reader from the beginning of the game to its final innings. The reader has been moved ahead to the real conflict of the article without missing anything of importance along the way. This summarization paragraph leads the reader to assume that the next scene will be a description of Mike's final moments in the game. And, of course, that's exactly what the article *will* focus on next.

The key thing about transitions is that they must logically direct the reader from one thought to the next in as subtle a manner as possible. Usually, the article itself will help you know which kind of transition to use at a given point. By observing what has been said thus far in your article, and by knowing the new direction you need to take, you can tell whether a correlation or summarization or some other technique would fit best.

FINDING ARTICLE IDEAS

We talked earlier about certain subjects which are especially popular with editors and readers. Those topics mentioned were not, however, the *only* topics that make for salable copy. There are literally hundreds of additional subjects which can be made into topics for feature stories.

Finging topics for features is quite easy, once you know how to go about searching for them. Here are some suggestions to assist you in your search.

- Check your local and area newspapers for small news items which you can develop into long feature stories for a different medium. You will need to do additional legwork and research, but it will be worth it when the small item you read in your morning paper later becomes a cover story by you in a national magazine.

- Listen to radio and TV news broadcasts and find a national news item that you can write up from a local angle. For example, if it is announced that Agent Orange causes cancer, find ex-servicemen in your hometown who came in contact with that defoliant in Vietnam and interview them to see if they have had reactions to it or not.

- Ask for topics to write about. Whenever an insurance agent finishes selling you a policy, he asks for a referral to someone else. You can do the same thing. Whenever you finish interviewing someone for a feature article, just ask, "Do you have any friends, relatives or colleagues who are involved in anything newsworthy which I might be able to write about?" Many times these people will give you several names of interesting people they know well.

- Use the Yellow Pages of your telephone book to find article ideas and news sources:

    (1) Send a postcard to all of the 'Associations" and "Organizations" listed and ask to be added to their mailing list for bulletins, newsletters and press releases. These will give you several news tips.

    (2) Check display ads for companies ready to celebrate their 25th or 50th anniversary in business and then write profiles of them.

(3) Find businesses that offer unusual services (musket repair, fortune cookie making, home radar installation) and write about them.

(4) Develop new slants on routine businesses. For example, what is the most valuable possession ever transported by the local armored truck company? Do any local florists sell meat-eating plants, such as Venus Fly Traps? Are Army surplus stores catering to modern doomsayers?

(5) Combine two topics: a report on the local egg producers and a report on local hog raisers could become, "Ham and Eggs: The Breakfast Business."

- Go to the library and read through the reference book *Facts on File.* It will tell you what the big news stories of previous years were. You then can do update features on those topics. Examples: "Are People Still Searching For Their Roots?" or "A Look at the Elvis Legend One Decade After Presley's Death."

PREPARING QUERIES

Most freelance writers contact magazine editors with a query letter before they begin the actual writing of a feature article. The query letter is a single-spaced one page letter that presents the idea for a potential feature article which the writer hopes to sell to the editor. Often, if an editor likes the idea presented in the query, he will not only give the go-ahead signal to prepare the article, but also offer suggestions for its length, style and research.

When writing a query letter, check the masthead of a current issue of the magazine you intend to contact, find the listing for the editor and send your letter to him or her by name rather than simply to "The Editor." If you've been published in other newspapers or magazines, send along a few tearsheets (samples) of your work.

Make sure that your article idea is unique. Look at back issues of the magazine to discover whether your topic has already been covered. And be sure that your article idea is appropriate for the magazine you are contacting. Don't send a profile of a

Republican candidate to a Democratic house organ or a feature on dieting to a magazine which features gourmet recipes.

Make your query letter lively, enthusiastic and positive. Be sure that your grammar is correct, your spelling is perfect and your typing is clear and clean.

Mention any autobiographical material that may be directly pertinent to the topic of the article. For example, if you are interested in writing an article about corporal punishment in the classroom, it will impress an editor if you mention that you are the mother of two elementary school children and that you are a licensed schoolteacher with fourteen years experience. Obviously, your background would give you special qualifications for writing that article.

When you finish the letter, briefly thank the editor and sign off. Don't add any notes of false flattery ("I'm a loyal subscriber to your magazine and I love every page of it") or ridiculous encouragement ("Print my article and I guarantee it will sell thousands of copies of your next issue"). As with a manuscript, enclose a self-addressed stamped envelope (S.A.S.E.) with all queries.

SUMMARY

Feature writing is one of the most enjoyable and lucrative ways in which freelance writers can expand the range of their writing outlets. There are more than 5,000 regional and national magazines which buy and print freelance feature articles. The range of topics they cover is vast.

By following the procedures presented in this chapter for finding feature article ideas, contacting editors, researching and writing, and then submitting manuscripts, you can begin now to enter this intriguing phase of freelance writing.

— Dennis E. Hensley

CHAPTER SIX

THEMES OF NONFICTION WRITING

In the past several decades there has been a change in the composition of our mass market magazines. Where formerly they contained as much fiction as nonfiction, the trend now is toward a preponderance of nonfiction. This is not to say that the trend might not reverse itself in the future. Nevertheless, it is altogether possible that new writers may more readily get a nonfiction article or book published than fiction. There are also hundreds of trade and business publications, religious magazines and regional magazines, all of which are in the market primarily for nonfiction.

Perhaps this emphasis on nonfiction is an outgrowth of the perilous times in which we live. Our twentieth century, with all its technological progress, is a century of barbarism where one holocaust has followed another. From Hitler to Reverend Jim Jones, the events reported by our newspapers and our broadcast media underscore the aphorism that "truth is stranger than fiction." Many editors and publishers feel that nonfiction is more salable than fiction.

THE NONFICTION ARTICLE

The pragmatic situation the beginning writer faces is that most articles for large circulation magazines are either staff written or written on assignment. Obviously, a magazine that has a weekly, monthly or quarterly deadline cannot depend on unsolicited material to fill its needs. Yet, there are thousands of magazines publishing tens of thousands of articles each year, and material by new writers is constantly being published.

The new writer must first realize that there is a basic difference between submitting fiction and submitting nonfiction. A short story should be submitted in its entirety. Nonfiction, however, is almost always preceded by a query letter. The difference is that the short story depends wholly on the talent and imagination of the writer; the nonfiction article may often sell on the basis of its new or startling information rather than its literary value. If you were to write an article about a simple way for millions of taxpayers to save hundreds of dollars on their tax returns, you can be sure that readers would appreciate your article even if the prose was less than brilliant. But article writing must not be substandard. On the contrary, the finest articles read like the finest fiction, in the sense that they embody all the elements of suspenseful storytelling. But the emphasis in nonfiction is on the subject.

The mechanics of feature writing have been discussed in the previous chapter. In the following table of categories for nonfiction articles, I have noted specific examples of articles published by my students which I hope may inspire you to go and do likewise.

How-To

Probably the most popular magazine articles are the *how-to's*, which cover every facet of our lives from how to repair a television set to how to improve one's love life. We are all interested in how to save money and how to better our lives. How-to articles on personal finance are particularly in great demand today because of the confused state of our economy.

A former student of mine whose hobby is woodworking is now writing a column for a weekly newspaper on how to repair furniture at little or no cost.

A particularly delightful how-to article was written and sold by another of my students. Neighbors who dropped in to see the young lady were always complimenting her on the beauty of her avocado plants. They were all growing avocado plants indoors, but none could match hers. What was her secret? With a charming smile, she told them she spoke lovingly to her plants. They were living beings to her and she gave them not only water and sunshine but also loving words. Her article was written with much warmth and humor.

How-to articles may provide a public service, too. Such topics as how to organize a political campaign to unseat undesirable politicians or how to organize neighborhoods to offer protection for children who may be in danger of being molested can generate public interest and personal action.

The how-to genre may also encompass the success story. How someone made a million dollars in real estate with little or no investment would provide not only an intriguing personality profile but also several tips on how to invest in property.

Hobbies and crafts offer a wealth of material for articles and books on how to do needlepoint, weave, sculpt, paint, create ceramics. The possibilities are infinite.

Travel

Millions of Americans travel each year both overseas and within the borders of our own United States. There are several magazines devoted solely to travel, such as *Travel and Leisure, Travel/Holiday,* and those published by auto clubs, such as *AAA World.* Sunday editions of metropolitan newspapers feature travel sections. Most of the articles are either staff written or written on assignment, but there are some opportunities for the newcomer.

I strongly suggest that the writer who has not previously written a travel article obtain copies of travel magazines or read the newspaper travel sections analytically.

Many of my students have travelled extensively and have been inspired to write about their experiences. The problem is that most of them have written their articles with a "gee whiz" approach, as if they were the first ones to set foot in Dublin or Paris or New Delhi, forgetting the thousands upon thousands of tourists who have already been there and have enjoyed the same experiences the writer encountered. Nothing new was added by the writer.

Most travel articles provide basic information: where to stay, which are the finest or most reasonable restaurants, how to anticipate climate variations, where to find recreational facilities and what travel restrictions may be in force. Some of the articles may include a brief history of the area, including two or three amusing anecdotes.

Some writers, like Horace Sutton, have spent a lifetime traveling and have turned the recording of those travels into a profitable occupation by becoming travel columnists and editors. Other writers have turned out a series of guidebooks.

The beginning writer should go beyond the general run of travel articles on which the editor depends. Perhaps discovering a part of London or Rome or Brussels that is off the beaten tourist track and well worth the traveler's time would intrigue an editor.

Another student of mine paid most of his expenses by writing travel articles about his family vacations, some of which were taken by trailer in the continental United States. He showed how a family of four could have a wonderful time at a relatively low cost.

Historical

History buffs abound and historical materials are available to all of us. Let me point out, at the outset, that this very availability is what makes writing the historical article hazardous, unless you are working on assignment. This is because historical material is in the public domain, which means that a dozen writers might be researching the same subject at the same time. You have an edge only if you have documents that are privately held.

Many history magazines want primary sources; that is, they prefer material not already in history books, encyclopedias or biographical dictionaries. A student of mine, for example, had letters written by one of her forebears, an aide to William Walker, the American adventurer who for a time ruled Nicaragua. Perhaps if you have an historical bent, you have already ransacked your attic or kept notes of the fabulous storeis told to you by your parents or grandparents.

Nonetheless, a great many historical articles are written based on secondary sources. I came across the story of Belva Lockwood in the *Dictionary of American Biography* and was intrigued by the accomplishments of this woman. Yet, whenever I asked my students whether they had ever heard of Belva Lockwood, the answer was invariably no. When I questioned their familiarity with the name Elizabeth Cady Stanton, the affirmative response was almost unanimous.

Mrs. Lockwood had twice run for president of the United States at a time when women could not vote. She was the first female lawyer to be permitted to argue a case before the United States Supreme Court. She campaigned all her adult life for women's suffrage, equal rights, justice for the Indians and international peace. I felt that Belva had been sadly neglected, so I obtained all available material from the Niagara County Historical Society in upstate New York, where she was born. My article was published by *Woman's Life.*

Regional magazines are often interested in tidbits of history relating to their areas of coverage. There are at least 20 magazines, both popular and scholarly, devoted to history. Daily and/or weekly newspapers and Sunday sections may be approached for possible articles tying in with anniversary dates of historic personages who lived or were born in the circulation area.

Religious/Inspirational

Sometime in our lives, unless we are outright atheists, we have experienced an act of faith. Perhaps a loved one given up for lost makes a miraculous recovery; or a family about to break up suddenly renews itself. Religious magazines do not want their writers to preach, but they do want them to inspire, teach and demonstrate that faith and prayer may often succeed where science or logic fails. One need not be of a particular faith to write for a denominational magazine.

Subjects may vary from describing new ways of raising funds for a church function to controversial issues that affect the contemporary church member. One of the participants in my writing workshops concentrated on the religious field. She had begun her career by writing book reviews for the local church paper. Within a year's time she had sold twenty articles to religious magazines, one of them discussing her views on the ordination of women. (See Dennis Hensley's sidebar in this chapter for tips on how to write for Christian periodicals.)

Humorous

It takes a certain genius to write good humorous articles on a regular basis. There are very few Russell Bakers or Art Buchwalds or Erma Bombecks. But there is humor in all our lives; witness the thousands of contributions to the *Reader's Digest* for "Life in These United States," "Humor in Uniform," "Campus Comedy" and "All in a Day's Work."

Tips on Writing Nonfiction Articles for Christian Periodicals

#1. Keep your article between 1,000 and 2,500 words long.

#2. Provide pragmatic, useful information.

#3. Offer a religious slant, but don't overindulge in theology.

#4. Avoid churchology vocabulary ("born again," "glory hallelujah") unless it is a general term ("tithe," "stewardship").

#5. Don't try to bend Scripture verses to fit some topic. If what you are writing about has no Bible reference (skydiving, auto repair), just present it straight forward.

#6. Remember that Christian readers expect a solution to a problem to come about through Divine intervention (through prayer, Bible reading or other means) combined with practical actions (based on biblical tenents).

#7. The article's tone should be upbeat yet familiar. Anecdotes, dialogue and good description appeal to editors.

#8. Research should be meticulous.

#9. Scan your newspaper to find topics of a controversial nature (gun control, genetic engineering, euthanasia) which you can research and write from a Christian perspective.

#10. Editors eagerly want people-oriented articles: personal dramas, interviews, uplifting incidents, real-life personal accounts, celebrity profiles and historial biographical sketches.

— Dennis E. Hensley

To illustrate the writer's ability to capitalize on a humorous incident, let me briefly outline an article written and sold by one of my students. Her family of six children presented a problem every time she and her husband wanted to take the family visiting or on a picnic. She decided that a van was the solution, but since funds were limited, she induced her husband to accompany her to an Army surplus sale. As it happened, the only two vehicles for sale that day were ambulances. Husband and wife looked at each other, smiled, bid and drove home an ambulance, feeling both self-conscious and foolish. It turned out they had made a remarkable investment. On their first trip to visit friends, they found that all vehicles gave them the right of way. When they parked their vehicle in their friend's driveway, the friend was suddenly besieged by phone calls and visits from neighbors anxious to know what the emergency was. My student realized the humor of the situation and its potential and so turned it into an hilarious article. As a bonus, the magazine to which she sold it asked her to write a sequel about the odds and ends one could purchase at an Army surplus sale.

Science/Medicine

Scientific topics are generally subjects where expertise is highly important. It is generally doctors who write about diets and scientists who write about nuclear energy. But it can be a fertile field for the freelance writer who has curiosity and a love for research, or the writer who is stimulated by a personal experience. Coauthorship projects with doctors are also possible.

One of my students learned that her son was having problems at school. His teacher said that the child read below grade level. It puzzled his mother because she knew her son was bright. Then one day the boy tried out for the Little League baseball team and was placed in center field. When the ball was hit to him, he ran toward it. It looked like an easy catch, but when the ball came close to him, he stood there bewildered and the ball plopped to the ground. With a shock, his mother realized the trouble was his vision.

That incident was the catalyst for her research into visual therapy to find a cure for her son. She found the cure, but in the process ran into a raging controversy between optometrists and ophthalmologists. She also discovered that thousands of youngsters faced the same problem as her son. Her research formed the basis for an article and, later, a booklet.

Profile

Most of the mass market circulation magazines feature interviews or profiles of nationally prominent people. These are invariably written on assignment because it generally takes an experienced reporter to gain access to a famous person. However, there are many opportunities for the beginning writer to interview local people who have an unusual story or who have made a unique contribution.

Some time ago, I wrote a profile of Gwynn Garnett for *Northern Virginia People* magazine. Garnett had a farm in Remington, Virginia, where he raised cattle organically; that is, the animals were given no drugs, and no pesticides were used on the pasture in which they grazed. This reduced the possibility of carcinogenic substances appearing in the cattle meat. Garnett won the support of many small cattle-raisers, and soon there were lines of consumers waiting to buy his meat. That would have made a story in itself, but when I interviewed Garnett, I discovered that he had a fascinating history. Before establishing his farm in Remington, he had spent many years and had many adventures attempting to introduce his cattle-raising system in Nigeria, the Congo and Iran. I sent a brief synopsis of Garnett's story to the magazine and received an immediate assignment. Regional magazines are receptive to profiles of local residents who have contributed to the welfare of the community.

Seasonal

Practically all the major magazines publish articles relating to holidays and to the various seasons. Because editors know they are going to feature Easter, Thanksgiving or Christmas articles, they will assign specific articles to established writers. It is therefore advisable if you have an idea for a Christmas article, let us say, to be sure that it will have a "shelf life" of more than one year. The rationale is that even though the magazine has already made an assignment, it could conceivably purchase your article, if it were that good, for the following year.

Seasonal articles must be submitted long in advance, at least six to nine months prior to publication. You may not feel in the Christmas mood in April, but you will have to project your imagination.

One of my students decided to do a series on holiday recipes that not only tasted good but also looked festive. She included ethnic holidays such as the Greek Easter. For each holiday she interviewed a woman who had a special holiday recipe. A metropolitan newspaper bought six of her articles.

The advantage of selling seasonal features to daily newspapers is that they do not require the long lead time of magazines.

Sports

Most articles on sports are seasonal: baseball in the spring, football in the fall. This is a specialized field dominated largely by established sports writers. There are possibilities for the freelance writer, however. For example, a student of mine wrote about the local high school girls' soccer team whose winning record earned it wide recognition and an opportunity to play in national tournaments. The article was published by *Young World.* So, look for the small but interesting local sports stories.

Personal Experience

Articles of this type do not follow the general rule for non-fiction; that is, they should be written and submitted in their entirety rather than preceded by a query letter.

The problem (the conflict) must be adequate. The experience one writes about must be exciting, heartwarming, humorous, or inspirational; anything but mundane.

A woman in one of my classes submitted a personal experience article about which she was very hesitant. She said it had taken her almost a year before she could bring herself to write it. My classroom methodology is to take manuscripts home with me for analysis. I then read the manuscripts aloud to the class. (This method gives the authors a new insight into their writing and also involves the entire class in a critique session.) When I read her manuscript to the class, there was a hushed silence. The personal experience concerned her daughter, who at fifteen was a beautiful girl, stood at the head of her class in grades, had a steady stream of boyfriends, in short, everything to make a teenager happy. But she was stricken with leukemia, and in six months she was dead.

What her mother described was an act of faith. It took her a year to recover from the shock. The writing itself, poignantly expressed, was a form of therapy. At first there was the inevitable question: why has this child, who had everything to live for, been taken from me? Then came the months of adjustment and the renewal of faith. The article was subsequently sold to a woman's magazine.

Often the mass circulation magazines will invite personal experience articles on subjects such as working mothers adjusting to careers and maintaining homes. Magazines dealing with the "new woman" are interested in personal experiences ranging from single parenthood to sexual harassment in the office. The personal experience of a father fighting for custody of his children in a divorce court will find an audience.

Scholarly/Professional

There are numerous scholarly and professional journals which offer an outlet for intellectual essays. This is not a field for the average freelance writer but rather for experts to expound on theories or present new discoveries in the areas of their expertise.

I believe we can obtain an insight into these scholarly journals by sampling a representative few and noting their requirements.

American Educator: Articles on current problems in education, professional ethics, social issues relevant to education, new trends in education.

North Carolina Historical Review: Articles concerning Southern history, particularly North Carolina history.

Journal of Modern Literature: Essays on 20th-century literature.

Columbia Journalism Review: In-depth articles and critical essays on the media.

Behavioral Medicine: Articles for physicians on behavioral techniques.

Progressive Architecture: Devoted to architects; articles include studies of interior design and urban design.

Trade/Business

There are probably more opportunities for writers in the Trade/Business magazines simply because they are the most numerous category. Almost any business activity one can think of has a publication devoted to that activity.

Some years ago, Larston Farrar, a freelance writer, wrote a book on how to earn a good living writing nonfiction articles. He placed the emphasis on turning out numerous short pieces for the Trade/Business magazines rather than concentrating on the mass circulation magazines. He found that while he might sell an article once every two months to a mass circulation magazine, he could sell three or four short articles every week to the Trade/Business magazines. In the aggregate he made more money from those limited circulation magazines than he did from the mass circulation magazines.

NONFICTION BOOKS

The preceding themes for nonfiction articles apply equally to nonfiction books. Many authors have expanded their articles into books, and many editors at publishing houses have read an article in a magazine and asked the author to develop it into a book.

Perhaps the case history of one of my students in getting a nonfiction book published may be of value to you. He was a history buff particularly engrossed in the events of the Civil War. He was aware that Civil War buffs are very numerous; witness the success of the *Civil War Times Illustrated* magazine. He knew also that the metropolitan Washington, D.C., area abounds in Civil War monuments and historic sites. He, therefore, made a survey of all the Civil War memorials in the area and researched available photographs and drawings at the National Archives, the Library of Congress and the Smithsonian Institution.

He decided he was going to develop a unique guide book entitled *Mr. Lincoln's City.* It would not only picture the historic sites and give directions to each but would include dramatic sketches describing briefly and vividly the action which made that site historic. His book was published and has been selling steadily. Because of its success, his publisher has contracted with him to prepare a similar guide book on the city of Richmond, Virginia, and its role in the Civil War.

— Stanley Field

CHAPTER SEVEN

DEVELOPING SHORT STORIES AND NOVELS

Paul R. Reynolds, one of the top literary agents and author of *The Writing and Selling of Fiction,* states that "anyone of reasonable intelligence can learn to write publishable nonfiction. About fiction, no such statement can be made." He goes on to say that success as a fiction writer requires talent, but "what this talent consists of is a mystery."

On the other hand, in noting the 50th anniversary of the prestigious Avery and Jule Hopwood awards in creative writing, the University of Michigan issued this statement: "The best student writers have been challenged to excel in their craft . . . . And one philosophical argument has been settled: Writing can be learned and good teaching can give depth and precision to that learning."

THE SHORT STORY

We can take a practical step toward that learning by setting down certain guidelines for writing the short story. There are no magic formulas for writing fiction. But there is a learning process, a need to start with the fundamentals.

In light of what is being published today, it is difficult to define a short story. Nowadays, there is a proliferation of literary magazines that publish the bulk of short stories, and many of the stories appearing in those magazines are no more than incidents, character sketches, or vignettes. Many of the literary magazines prefer the experimental story, breaking away from the traditional type, perhaps in the same manner that modern art has deviated from representational art. Erskine Caldwell, in a preface to his short story, "Warm River" (*This is My Best,* edited by Whit Burnett, Doubleday) offered this brief commentary:

> The writing of a short story can be a dangerous adventure. What makes it dangerous may be the mis-guided belief of a writer that he is obligated to tell a story. And, when this design is followed, the structure

is sure to be a contrived plot garishly colored with the gaudy crayons of the topical and sensational.

But the short story can be more than this. It can be the explicit expression of a casual feeling or a deep emotion when, in conflict or with sympathy, two or more persons act in response to the desires and motivations of the mind and heart. Although it is evasive and not always successfully attained, this is the essence of fiction that writers of durable reading seek to implant in their works.

In the learning process, I believe the beginning writer should start with the traditional story; that is, one which has a beginning, a middle and an end; one that presents a problem and concludes with the resolution of that problem. The mass circulation magazines, which incidentally are the highest paying, generally prefer the traditional approach.

The Significant Problem

In planning a story, consider, first of all, the problem or conflict the protagonist is going to face. Determine whether the problem is an important one which will catch the attention of many readers and be of universal significance.

For example, divorce presents an important conflict, a breakdown in family relations. One may say that divorce is now so common it no longer presents a real problem. But a professor of psychology at the University of California made a study of the ten most severe traumas that affect people. He found that the death of a loved one headed the list, but *second* on the list was divorce. Therefore, no matter how prevalent divorce may be, it still presents a highly traumatic situation; in other words, a significant problem. The fact that divorce is so widespread also means that it is a universal problem and, hence, can be used for many short stories.

Involved Relations

After creating a realistic, significant conflict for the protagonist, it is necessary to build a series of complications in which to involve the character. Keep the story building to a climax. If the climax comes too early or the ending is too obvious, the reader will soon lose interest. Start with a minor crisis and build to a major crisis. Try to sustain a major crisis that appears to be unresolvable or insurmountable, a point in your story where readers will say to themselves, "How in the world is she going to get out of that situation!"

Viewpoint

Because the short story is "short," it should be told from a single viewpoint. Whose story is it: the mother's, the father's, the son's, the daughter's, the fiance's? The short story does not have the scope of the novel, and too many viewpoints could be confusing. If there are several major characters, it would be difficult to achieve a full realization of those characters within the confines of a short story.

Motivation

The primary reason given by magazine editors for the rejection of short stories is lack of clear character motivation. An author must induce in the reader the "suspension of disbelief." No matter what the subject is, even the supernatural, readers must be involved to the extent that they believe what is happening. Motivation — what makes the characters tick — helps to maintain the reality.

In his book, *Character and Conflict,* Professor Alvin B. Kernan defines a motive as "the force that moves a person to seek the satisfaction of some need." Writers, he adds, "should attempt to discover the fundamental motive that finds expression in everything the character does."

Consider your own motivations. What causes you to react as you do in certain situations? What do you think made a friend or relative act the way he or she did? What are the emotions that motivate people? Ambition? Greed? Fear? Love? Hate? Lust? Joy? Sorrow?

Think of the great short stories and you will quickly recall that each of their main characters had a definite motivation for his or her actions. In Jack London's "To Build a Fire" the greenhorn goes into the barren cold by himself because of his *arrogance* in wanting to prove the old sourdoughs wrong in their belief that no

100

one should travel alone in the Yukon. This arrogance costs the greenhorn his life, but it is very believable to the reader.

Similarly, in O. Henry's "The Gift of the Magi," it is an *overwhelming love* that motivates the wife to sell her pretty hair and the husband to sell his gold watch to raise money to buy Christmas presents for each other.

Plausibility

Another factor that adds realism to any story is plausibility.

Suppose the story requires a courtroom scene. If you happen to be a lawyer who also writes, you will be familiar with courtroom procedure. But not many professional writers are lawyers. To familiarize yourself with legal procedures you can do either "live" or library research. "Live" research might entail asking a lawyer friend for details of courtroom procedure or observing one or two trials in progress. Library research involves, of course, the reading of books about courtroom procedure.

Again, if the story concerns the serious illness of the protagonist, you can ask your doctor about medical procedures or you can study a medical encyclopedia.

It is not necessary to be clinical in your approach. Too many details may demonstrate your erudition, but bore your reader. Still, you need to know enough and show enough in your story to make it plausible.

Few writers can or want to experience every facet of life, particularly painful situations. If you are writing a short story about someone who is jailed for a crime, you hardly want to spend time behind bars in order to write realistically about prisoners. This is where the writer's imagination and talent come in. A novelist like Stephen Crane could write that classic of Civil War stories, *The Red Badge of Courage,* before he had ever experienced the traumas of war as a correspondent in Cuba during the Spanish-American conflict. Crane was able to describe the emotions of men in combat even before he had ever witnessed any combat firsthand. He gave his battle scenes in *The Red Badge of Courage* the semblance of truth. All good fiction writing must have verisimilitude or else the reader will not become caught up in the reality of the conflict.

101

Characterization

One assignment I always give to my students is to write a brief biography of the protagonist of their proposed story. This shows the students how well they know their hero or heroine. If knowledge of the protagonist is superficial, the characterization will be superficial. There may be details in the biography which may never appear in the story, but these details will help the writer to more fully understand the fictional character. A story may begin when the protagonist is forty years old and a successful businessman, but an action he takes may be motivated by some incident that occurred during his childhood. The author should be familiar with the protagonist's childhood. What sort of child was he? What was his relationship with his parents? What sort of education did he have? What were his economic circumstances? What were his sexual inclinations? All these factors will help the writer create, literally and figuratively, a full-bodied character.

Some years ago, a series of television beer commercials featured a duo known as Bert and Harry. The commercials were extraordinarily successful and won the coveted *Clio* award, comparable to Hollywood's *Oscar.* When I interviewed the writers of the commercials, they showed me the 25-page biographies they had written of Bert and Harry. Those two *commercial* characters came alive even in the brief minute they were allotted for their dialogue. Viewers spoke of them as real people; and this was directly attributable to the background work done by the writers.

Professional writers, in any area of writing, work hard at their craft and take time to develop methods which will help them tell their story most effectively.

Remember always that fictional characters should be multi-dimensional. All of us are. How many times have you said to yourself, "I never thought he or she was that sort of person." In other words, that person showed a dimension that was totally new to you. We are none of us wholly good nor wholly bad. Years ago, Hollywood producers, particularly of western movies, used one-dimensional devices to differentiate the hero from the villain. The hero always wore a white hat and rode a white horse. The villain wore a black hat and rode a black horse. Today that sort of device would only inspire laughter. The westerns of today are called adult westerns; they try to bring more dimension (and therefore more believability) to their characters.

There is a word we must bear in mind when creating protagonists and that word is "sympathy." If your protagonists are not sympathetic, your readers will not care what happens to them. Even if your main characters are villains, they must engender some sympathy. Scrooge may be the best known villain in all literature, but by the end of Dickens' *A Christmas Carol,* he has won our sympathy.

We can make our characters easy for the reader to visualize by describing their physical appearance: hair color, eye color, shape of the nose, body build. Do they have any noticeable blemishes or scars? Do they use any distinctive gestures? What sort of clothes do they wear?

We learn about people from the way they speak. A college graduate will have a more polished speech than an illiterate. An immigrant will speak English with an accent.

We also learn about people from the way others speak about them. A wife may characterize her husband as lovable. A secretary may describe her supervisor as a cold fish. However, a word of caution: people are often biased against other people and their comments may reflect their bias. It may be that we learn more about the character of the people uttering the comments than the one commented upon.

There are several questions writers should ask themselves in regard to characterization. Why do the characters have their peculiar personal and social problems? What motivates them to act as they do? Are they responsible for their actions?

Characterization may move in two main directions: (1) the protagonist we meet at the beginning of the story does not change by the end, that is, the forces brought into play in the story produce no effect on the protagonist; (2) the incidents of the story and the resolution of the problem do effect a change in the protagonist.

Dialogue

It is possible to write a short story with no dialogue, like Leroi Jones' "The Screamers," or as a monologue, like John Barth's "Night-Sea Journey," or with a bare minimum of dialogue, like Carson McCuller's "The Ballad of the Sad Cafe." The optimum, however, is a mixture of narrative and dialogue. The writer can test dialogue by reading it aloud to hear the sound of it. After all, dialogue represents the spoken word.

Dialogue should be relevant to the story and it must advance the action. You must avoid the boring (unless you are depicting a character as a bore). In our daily lives our conversations are, unfortunately, more mundane than scintillating. We need to include some of the amenities when our characters meet, but we need not mimic such amenities as they occur in our daily greetings. For instance, you may meet a friend on the street and your conversation may go something like this:

"Hello. How are you?"

"I'm fine. How are you?"

"I'm fine. Nice day."

"Yeah, if it doesn't rain."

"Rain?"

"Yeah. Paper says twenty percent chance."

"Hmm. How's everything going?"

"Fine. How's everything going with you?"

"Fine."

And so on, and so on, ad nauseum, obviously alienating the reader.

There is no harm in letting the dialogue wander as you write the first draft. It is more important to complete the story, then to go over it meticulously and eliminate the deadwood. Let the

104

characters say hello to each other, and from then on their conversation should be interesting and informative.

You must identify the speakers in your story. You may be able to write ten lines of dialogue without identification, especially if the characters have distinct speech patterns. But if your people come from similar backgrounds and you have long stretches of dialogue without identification, very soon readers will find themselves stopping to count back to discover who's speaking to whom.

Most professional writers use one verb for identification, to the exclusion of others: said. He said. She said. The use of a multitude of verbs such as "she murmured," "he asserted," "she observed," "he commented" are usually signs of the novice writer. What's important is what's between the quotation marks. At times you will have to use a qualifying verb when you want your characters to sound sarcastic or ironic. If you write, "That's very nice of you," she said, the reader will accept the statement literally. But if you write, "That's very nice of you," she said sarcastically, it will give the line of dialogue a completely different interpretation. In speaking, an inflection can change the meaning of a statement. But in a fictional account, the reader has only the printed word to go by; therefore, if the author intends a character's remark to be taken either warmly or facetiously, he or she must so indicate.

There is another simple and direct method of identifying the speaker, one we use all the time in our daily conversations: our names. Your character may say, "I'll not speak of it again, Herbert." And further on in the dialogue, Herbert may say, "We've gone over this a dozen times, Margaret."

Listen to people closely. Note that most of us speak idiomatically. We use contractions. Therefore you should use contractions in your dialogue. We don't generally say, "I am going to the store." We say, "I'm going to the store." Not using a contraction may give a completely different emphasis to a statement. For example, take the sentence, "You'll go to the meeting, Joe." That is a simple direct statement. But if Joe doesn't want to go to the meeting and has to be urged, the dialogue would read, "You *will* go to the meeting, Joe."

105

Also, not using contractions may be a form of characterization. Let us say one of the characters is a foreigner who has learned English at school. She has probably been taught grammatically rather than conversationally and therefore she will not speak idiomatically and may often sound stilted. This may be indicated by the preciseness of the dialogue.

Another element you may have to contend with is dialect. "Don't overdo dialect," should be a cardinal rule for writers. The reader should be given the flavor of the dialect, not an exact transcription. Here is an example from a short story, "Play Up, Play Up and Get Tore In," by George MacDonald Fraser:

> "Wandered!" said the corporal bitterly afterwards. "Away wi' the fairies! He does that, and for the rest o' the game he micht as well be in his bed. He's a genius, sir, but no' near often enough. Ye jist daurnae risk 'im again."

Note that in the dialogue a good deal is written in standard English: "He does that, and for the rest . . . as well be in his bed. He's a genius, sir . . ." The flavor is there but the dialect needs no translation, which brings to mind a student who wrote a story about people living in the Ozarks. The woman was born there and was thoroughly familiar with the regionalisms. She transcribed the dialect so faithfully that it was impossible for the rest of the students to understand the dialogue. I recommended to the student that she read works by Mark Twain and John Steinbeck to see how the *flavor* of dialect can enhance dialogue.

Exposition

Fiction writers must constantly feed information to their readers: names of the characters, physical description, age, locale, occupations or avocations of the characters, the relationships of the characters to each other. The most talented writers bring this information to their readers within the movement of the story. It is the art that conceals art. A good dressmaker, for example, conceals the stitches. When we see the dress we should be aware of its elegance, not of the stitches that put it together.

Dialogue can serve as exposition. Suppose you are writing a scene depicting a man sitting in a restaurant obviously waiting for someone. A woman walks in, seats herself at his table and says, "Hello," a very normal greeting. But what does it tell us about the relationship of the man and woman? Nothing. Suppose when the woman seats herself, she says, "Hello, Uncle Ron," also a very normal greeting. The addition of "Uncle Ron" immediately clarifies the relationship between the two.

In Hamlin Garland's "The Return of a Private," we have an example of exposition in the opening paragraph.

> The nearer the train drew toward La Crosse, the soberer the little group of "vets" became. On the long way from New Orleans they had beguiled tedium with jokes and friendly chaff; or with planning with elaborate detail what they were going to do now, after the war. A long journey, slowly, irregularly, yet persistently pushing northward. When they entered on Wisconsin territory they gave a cheer, and another when they reached Madison, but after that they sank into dumb expectancy. Comrades dropped off at one or two points beyond, until there were only four or five left who were bound for La Crosse County.

We learn that the train is traveling from New Orleans carrying a group of war veterans, some of whom are on their way to La Crosse. We are also informed of the tedium of the journey.

Now witness the opening paragraph of Erskine Caldwell's short story, "Warm River."

> The driver stopped at the suspended footbridge and pointed out to me the house across the river. I paid him the quarter fare for the ride from the station two miles away and stepped from the car. After he had gone I was alone with the chill night and the star-pointed lights twinkling in the valley and the broad green river flowing warm below me. All around me the mountains rose like black clouds in the night, and only by looking straight heavenward could I see anything of the dim afterglow of sunset.

From this paragraph we learn nothing about the narrator. We do not know whether the narrator is male or female. We do know the narrator stopped at a footbridge but we don't know where it is located. We do not learn the name of the protagonist until the second page.

What the two foregoing examples illustrate is that all writers have their own ways of expressing themselves. Give the same idea to ten writers, and they will have ten different approaches. It only underscores the premise that there is no formula for creative writing. Creativity must be equated with originality. You can study techniques and decide to adopt one or another for your own writing, but if you have any talent at all you will express yourself in your own individual manner.

Devices

A common device writers employ for exposition is the flash-back, that is, going back in time to relate an incident that has an important bearing on the story. Some writers avoid using the flashback, preferring a chronological approach.

The flashback has been used as a device for relating a complete story. Thornton Wilder's *The Bridge of San Luis Rey* was told almost entirely in flashback. The story opens with a very dramatic sequence: Five Peruvians are making their way through the countryside and come to a bridge across a canyon, the famous bridge of San Luis Rey. As they cross the bridge, it collapses, sending them all to their deaths. The story reaches back into the lives of the five travelers and recounts how it came about that each one was on the bridge at the exact moment of its collapse.

Another illustration of a flashback is a memory sequence. Suppose a story opens with the heroine in New York. She is an executive for a large corporation. One day she sits musing at her desk, thinking that it is ten years now since she has left her home in a small town in the Midwest, ten years since she has last seen her parents. She decides she is going to take some time off to drive home.

When she arrives at her home, she parks her car, but before she gets out she gazes at the old familiar homestead. She recalls that day ten years ago when her parents and she were estranged. She had graduated from college and her parents had expected her to marry her childhood sweetheart to whom she was already engaged. They looked forward to having her live close by and one day having grandchildren. But she had felt stifled and limited and had wanted an opportunity to go off to expand her horizons. She broke here engagement and left her bewildered parents, knowing they had been hurt.

By means of this flashback memory sequence, the writer is able to inform the reader of the existing situation so that when the protagonist knocks at the door and her mother or father answers, the reader is prepared for and wondering what sort of confrontation will take place.

Coincidence

Coincidence occurs often in our daily lives. We decide, for no apparent reason, to shop today at Grand Union instead of Safeway and we meet an old friend we haven't seen in years. Although coincidence happens frequently, as a literary device it must appear logical; otherwise, an editor reading the story will say the coincidence sounds contrived.

To illustrate: suppose the story opens with a young woman running for a bus. She misses it and has to take the next bus. There is only one seat vacant on the bus. She sits down and discovers that the young man sitting next to her is an old friend from her hometown. During their conversation she reveals that she is divorced and has a couple of children. He tells her he is also divorced, and before she reaches her destination they plan to meet again. It could happen that way in life.

Now let us employ the same situation but insert a logical reason for the young woman to miss the bus. We can begin the story in the woman's apartment. Her baby sitter cannot come and she is frantically on the phone getting another. The delay in obtaining another sitter is what causes her to miss the bus.

In the first instance we are given no reason for her missing the bus. It is a contrived incident. In the second instance the reader is given a logical reason for the woman to miss the bus and the ensuing coincidence of meeting the man to occur.

It may seem paradoxical that fiction should be more logical than truth, but that only bears out the aphorism that truth is stranger than fiction.

Description

The question naturally arises: how much description, particularly of locale, is necessary? It all depends on the locale. If the story takes place in a typical suburban community in the United States, it may need little description. If the locale is foreign to readers, more detail is necessary to evoke the lifestyle of the people, the clothes they wear, the structure of their homes, even the layout of their streets; vivid portrayals are required so that the surroundings can be clearly envisioned. In a short story description should be succinct.

Resolution

We come now to the conclusion of the story, the resolution. Despite all of our sophistication, most readers still prefer the happy ending. That is why you will find that most stories in mass circulation magazines have upbeat endings.

Look at it this way: fiction, no matter how literary or serious in theme, should be entertaining. Somerset Maugham, in *The Art of Fiction,* states that "the aim of art is to please." Most people read fiction for enjoyment, not information. However, James Michener, one of our most successful writers, combines both in his fiction. He has stated that his goal is not only to entertain his readers but to inform them. Nevertheless, the majority of readers want enjoyable vicarious experiences from the stories they read, which include satisfactory resolutions to difficulty.

A story which ends happily is likely to find a much more receptive audience than one that doesn't. And there is another reason for the requirement for upbeat endings by mass circulation magazines. These magazines owe their financial existence to the advertisements they display. The number of advertisements is almost always in direct ratio to the number of subscribers, and the profit accrues from the advertisements, not the subscriptions. When you read *Redbook, McCall's, Ladies Home Journal, Good Housekeeping* or *Cosmopolitan,* you may start a story on, let us say, page 25, then you have to turn to page 32, then to page 43, and during the turning of those pages, your eyes automatically scan a number of advertisements. If you were depressed from having read a story with a downbeat ending in one of those magazines, psychologically you would not look with any enthusiasm at the advertisements. An upbeat, well resolved story will put you in a happy frame of mind, the editors reason, and you will then be prone to regard the advertisements with favor.

The happy ending is not a requisite for such magazines as *Harper's, Atlantic Monthly, New Yorker,* or for the 500 or more *literary* magazines which publish short stories. For those magazines, the emphasis is on quality. The *literary* magazines carry little or no advertising, and the advertising they do carry is mostly generated from university presses and small presses. Unfortunately, however, the circulation of literary magazines is very limited.

A point of clarification: I do not mean for you to avoid writing stories that have tragic endings. After all, Shakespeare's greatest plays are his tragedies. But we do want to emphasize the facts of publishing life.

It is possible, if you so desire, to write a story with an un-resolved ending, one in which the author leaves the resolution to the imagination of the reader. The classic example is Frank Stockton's, "The Lady or the Tiger." It tells the story of a bold youth who loves the king's daughter. He is condemned to open one of two doors. Behind one is a girl he must marry. Behind the other is a ferocious tiger. The king's daughter manages to learn the secret and she signals her lover to open one of the doors. The story ends there. We do not know the resolution she indicated. When first published, the story aroused a great deal of discussion. But the fact is there have been very few short stories written with unresolved endings. Most readers prefer a resolved ending.

Happy ending or not, in planning the resolution, be sure the conflict is resolved by the protagonist, not by some outside force. For example, if the protagonist is beset by mounting debts which will result in catastrophe unless the debts are paid promptly, don't resolve the situation by having a rich uncle die suddenly and leave the person a fortune. Have the protagonist, by dint of his or her own wits, discover the means to resolve the plight. A stronger story results when the protagonist solves his or her own problem.

The Opening Approach

I have chosen two selections not only to demonstrate how some of our most famous authors have begun their short stories but also to illustrate writing techniques which are of invaluable use to authors.

Here is the opening paragraph of "Children on Their Birthdays," by Truman Capote.

Yesterday afternoon the six-o'clock bus ran over Miss Bobbit. I'm not sure what there is to be said about it; after all, she was only ten years old, still I know no one of us in this town will forget her. For one thing, nothing she ever did was ordinary, not from the first time that we saw her, and that was a year ago. Miss Bobbit and her mother, they arrived on that same six-o'clock bus, the one that comes through from Mobile. It happened to be my cousin Billy Bob's birthday, and so most of the children in town were here at our house. We were sprawled on the front porch having tutti-frutti and devil cake when the bus stormed around Deadman's curve. It was the summer that never rained; rusted dryness coated everything; sometimes when a car passed on the road, raised dust would hang in the still air an hour or more. Aunt El said if they didn't pave the highway soon she was going to move down to the seacoast; but she'd said that for such a long time. Anyway, we were sitting on the porch, tutti-frutti melting on our plates, when suddenly, just as we were wishing that something would happen, something did; for out of the red road dust appeared Miss Bobbit. A wiry little girl in a starched, lemon-colored party dress, she sassed along with a grown-up mince, one hand on her hip, the other supporting a spinsterish umbrella. Her mother, lugging two cardboard valises and a wind-up victrola, trailed in the background. She was a gaunt shaggy woman with silent eyes and a hungry smile.

Reread that first sentence: "Yesterday afternoon the six-o'clock bus ran over Miss Bobbit." It is what we may term, idiomatically, a "grabber." It gains immediate attention. It is an excellent device for the traditional short story.

The next time you riffle through a magazine and then stop to read a particular story, ask yourself why that opening paragraph caught your attention. You will find exemplified in this and in the Eudora Welty selection below two different methods of approach, which only serve to illustrate again that creativity equates with originality. Writers, as I have noted, have different ways of expressing themselves. These successful authors all reach wide audiences, underscoring the point that there is no formula for creativity.

Now let us study other aspects of Capote's opening paragraph. He writes, "We were sprawled on the front porch having tutti-frutti and devil cake." He might have written, "having ice cream and cake." But he was using what we term *picture words*. Think of it this way. The brain, wonderful instrument that it is, transposes words into visual images. The more specific the picture words are, the clearer the image. There may be fifty varieties of ice cream and a hundred varieties of cake. With "ice cream and cake" you receive an image, but it's a blurred one. "Tutti-frutti" and "devil cake" are very specific and therefore more readily visualized. When the writer gives a very specific description of a character, the reader can *see* that person. When the writer describes a garden and says the shrubbery is lovely, it is a correct statement, but "shrubbery" gives a blurred image. When it is identified as "boxwood" or "yew," it evokes a clear image. Again, if the writer mentions "a grove of trees," the image is not clear. Be specific: oak trees, cedars, maples? Remember, the reader has only the printed words to go by; make them vivid.

Another device writers use is imagery. They create an image, a picture. Observe that Capote writes, "she sassed along with a grown-up mince." He could have written, "she walked," which is what she was doing. The imagery of "sassed along with a grown-up mince" gives a much more vivid picture of how she walked and an insight into the sort of person Miss Bobbit was.

The following paragraph is taken from Eudora Welty's short story, "A Worn Path."

It was December — a bright frozen day in the early morning. Far out in the country there was an old Negro woman with head tied in a red rag, coming along a path through the pinewoods. Her name was Phoenix Jackson. She was very old and small and she walked slowly in the dark pine shadows, moving a little from side to side in her steps, with the balanced heaviness and lightness of a pendulum in a grandfather clock. She carried a thin, small cane made from an umbrella, and with this she kept tapping the frozen earth in front of her. This made a grave and persistent noise in the still air, that seemed meditative like the chirping of a solitary little bird.

This opening paragraph is far different from Capote's. It has a quiet beginning. It attracts by its mood rather than by its impact. Curiosity is aroused by the Old Negro woman and where she is going.

In this one paragraph, Eudora Welty employs a great deal of imagery. There could have been a period after "moving a little from side to side in her steps." But the author adds "with the balanced heaviness and lightness of a pendulum in a grandfather clock." That imagery heightens our visual perception. Welty writes, "This made a grave and persistent noise in the still air." Again, the sentence could have ended there, but she gives us added vivid imagery: "that seemed meditative like the chirping of a solitary little bird."

We have seen how two different authors each use an individual approach to opening their stories. Perhaps this may seem somewhat confusing to the novice, but as I have stated, there is no formula for creative writing.

THE NOVEL

A few years ago I attended a writers' conference in Tarrytown, New York. The moderator was James Michener and the panelists consisted of senior executives of some of the foremost book publishers. What we discussed were the problems facing writers in getting novels published, particularly first novels. The publishers agreed that first novels were difficult to sell. But what then? Does one start with a second novel? Although it is true that a first novel by an unknown writer may not earn back its advance, it is also true that some first novels have become runaway best-sellers. One best seller for a publisher can easily recompense him for many commercial failures.

There was a consensus among the publishers present that a good book eventually will be published. Translated, that means a good book in the opinion of the publishers. Authors may believe they have written great novels, but if no publisher agrees, their books won't be published.

To his credit, Michener made the point, as he put it, "I won't live forever," and therefore it was incumbent on the publishers to encourage new talent. Most of the publishers stated that they would not read unsolicited novels. They insisted that novels must be submitted to them through agents. One publisher suggested that novelists send him a letter in which they "sell" their proposed books; in other words, they must arouse enough interest to make the publisher want to read the novel.

All this was prelude to the appearance of two new novelists, Marilyn Durham and Shelley List, who related their experiences in getting their first novels published. Their comments were directed to where ideas for their novels originated.

Marilyn Durham, the author of the very successful novel, *The Man Who Loved Cat Dancing,* said that she was a "writing freak." By this she meant that her experiences differed from those of most writers. She did not begin her writing until she was over forty. She had never written or published a work of fiction prior to her first novel. She did not draw on events in her personal life. She spent many hours in the local library, and her research led to the background material of the historical romance she was to write.

She sent the novel to several publishers, all of whom turned it down. She then obtained an agent who was favorably impressed by the manuscript and sold the book. It was also made into a motion picture starring Burt Reynolds and earned a great deal of money for Mrs. Durham.

The next speaker, Shelley List, author of *Did You Love Daddy When I Was Born,* and *Nobody Makes Me Cry,* described her experiences in writing her novels and how they managed to get published. She had written about 24 short stories, none of which were published. She then went to work for a movie fan magazine, which she found very interesting because it gave her the opportunity to meet many of the Hollywood entertainers. But the catalyst for her first novel was an intimate personal experience.

After many years of marriage, Shelley List went through a traumatic divorce. When a year or so had passed and the pain was somewhat eased, she decided to write about that experience. She knew millions of women were divorced every year and certainly must have explored in their minds the events leading to the termination of their marriage. This was what List set out to do: analyze the cumulation of incidents that led to the breakup; portray, in the form of a novel, a personal tragedy that was also a universal experience.

When the book was completed, List found an agent who was receptive but also critical of the manuscript. She suggested many revisions. Later, when the manuscript was sold, the editor also requested changes. It was a slow process and List discovered what all professional writers know: writing is largely rewriting.

Her second novel, *Nobody Makes Me Cry,* is also based on personal experience. After the divorce, her mother had come to live with her. Unfortunately, her mother was afflicted with terminal cancer. How an individual faces up to such a traumatic situation is the theme of List's second novel.

I have used the above illustrations to demonstrate how divergent are the subjects chosen by novelists. Durham delved into history for ideas. List's novels were based entirely on personal experience.

Thomas H. Uzzell, in *The Technique of the Novel,* offers some cogent advice to the would-be novelist:

> The story you most want to write is not necessarily the one you will handle best. Many a time I have heard writers brought up in small towns of the Middle West say, after living a year or so in New York, that they wanted to write stories or a novel about life in New York. When I suggested instead the life of their home-towns, they were eloquent in their distaste for the "sticks" from which they had "escaped"; it bored them; they wanted to forget it. They admitted that they had exhaustive knowledge of the people at home and had not yet learned their way around in the metropolis, but stubbornly they insisted that they wanted to write about the big city. I argued that good novels flowed from full knowledge rather than from more romantic

interest and dreams. The answer to this was: "But what can anyone say about such dull places?" My answer was: "You might explain why you find them dull." This was the theme of *Main Street,* the most successful novel of the first generation of this century.

A look at successful novelists and how they began their writing careers was offered by *Writer's Digest* in an article entitled "My First Sale" (December, 1981). Ray Bradbury, after eight years and many rejection slips, sold a short story. Arthur Hailey said his first published piece was a letter to the editor. Phyllis A. Whitney, after four years of rejections, finally sold a short story to the *Chicago Daily News.* They all became successful when they began to write about what they knew best.

Technique

The guidelines set forth in the preceding section, on the short story, can be applied to the novel as well, with modifications that take into account the specific requirements of the longer fiction form. First of all, the novel may average 100,000 words, whereas the short story may average 3,000 words. The novel provides a very large canvas on which to portray characters and manipulate a plot. I stressed that the short story should be told from a single viewpoint. Many novels do tell their story from the viewpoint of one person, but because the novel has such a broader scope, its story may encompass several viewpoints. Instead of one major character, a novel may have several major characters.

One successful novel uses nine different viewpoints. It opens with the murder of a business tycoon. There are nine suspects, and as the story unfolds, each one of the suspects gives an entirely different picture of the dead man: to his wife, he is a shallow, hateful person; to his mistress, a generous, passionate lover; to his lawyer, a conniver; to his banker, a brilliant financier, and so on.

In the matter of characterization, I discussed the value of writers preparing biographies of their major characters. Norman Mailer, in an interview for *Writers at Work,* said that for his novel, *The Naked and the Dead,* "I had a file full of notes and a long dossier on each man." Mailer created detailed histories for each of his characters and used these histories to make each character appear real to the reader.

First Person or Third Person?

One technique I have not previously discussed is the matter of whether to tell the story in the first person or the third person. Each method has its advantages.

The use of the first person helps to establish believability. It is as if you were listening to a friend relating what happened to him or her. Somerset Maugham, in *The Art of Fiction,* states that writing in the first person "lends verisimilitude to the narrative and obliges the author to stick to his point, for he can tell you only what he has himself seen, heard or done ... another advantage of using the first person is that it enlists your sympathy with the narrator." But a disadvantage of the method, Maugham goes on to say "is that the narrator when, as in *David Copperfield,* he is also the hero, cannot without impropriety tell you that he is handsome and attractive; he is apt to seem vainglorious when he relates his doughty deeds and stupid when he fails to see what is obvious to the reader, that the heroine loves him."

A more effective way of using the first person, as Maugham notes, is the example of Herman Melville's *Moby Dick.* Here the story is narrated by Ishmael, the former schoolmaster who signs on board the *Pequod* and meets Captain Ahab. It is Ahab's story which Ishmael relates. He can be objective about his portrayal of the hero.

Writing in the first person does not allow narrators to be omniscient. They cannot enter the minds of the other characters; they can only give their opinion of what the characters might be thinking. The narrators also have to be eyewitnesses to events or otherwise the authors must use the weak device of having one of the characters relate the events to the narrator. However, many great novels have been written in the first person: *Treasure Island* by Robert Louis Stevenson, *A Farewell to Arms* by Ernest Hemingway, *Cakes and Ale* by Somerset Maugham.

Most novelists prefer the third-person approach. By using the third person, novelists, figuratively, play God. They are privy to all their characters' thoughts; they are present at all scenes of action; they know everything there is to know about all their characters; they report all conversations verbatim. Writing in the third person permits novelists full, unfettered range. The leeway afforded by this method is advantageous to writers.

There has to be some intuitive feeling on the part of writers in choosing to tell their stories in the first or third person. Since most of Maugham's stories are based on incidents in his life or on people he met, it was natural for him to use the first-person technique in much of his fiction. But interestingly enough, Maugham's classic novel, *Of Human Bondage,* although largely autobiographical, was written in the third person.

Some writers have experimented with a mixture of the first and third person in their novels. In Steinbeck's *The Winter of Our Discontent,* the first two chapters are written in the third person; then, beginning with the third chapter, a switch is made to the first person.

Chapter One opens as follows: "When the fair cold morning of April stirred Mary Hawley awake, she turned over to her husband and saw him, little fingers pulling a frog mouth at her."

Chapter Three begins: "My wife, my Mary, goes to her sleep the way you would close the door of a closet. So many times, I have watched her with envy."

There are four shifts of viewpoint in this Steinbeck novel: It opens in the third person, changes to the first, then back to the third person and returns to the first. This is confusing to the reader and certainly *The Winter of Our Discontent* is judged one of Steinbeck's weaker novels.

In William Styron's highly praised novel, *Sophie's Choice,* we have a more successful example of transposition from first to third person. The opening chapter is autobiographical and lends itself to the first person technique, but when the narrator meets Sophie and she begins to tell him her life's tragic history, Styron switches from first to third person.

There is a very apparent rationale for Styron to employ this method. If he used the first person throughout, he would have to have Sophie continuously relating what happened to her. Instead, he has Sophie start to tell part of her history, but the chapter immediately following is written in the third person. In that way we are shown what happened to Sophie, for example, in the concentration camp, rather than having her tell about it. A story has more impact when we are with the characters as the events occur rather than being told about what transpired.

Styron employs a simple but effective device for transposing from first to third person. In Chapter Nine, he writes, "Poland is a beautiful heart wrenching soul-split country which in many ways (I came to see through Sophie's eyes and memory that summer, and through my own eyes in later years) resembles or conjures up images of the American South." That parenthetical statement tells us in effect that the author/narrator is going to reconstruct an episode of Sophie's life as she revealed it. The reconstruction of the episode is accomplished in Chapter Ten.

Chapter Thirteen uses a somewhat similar device: "I must now set down a brief vignette which I have tried to refashion from the outpouring of Sophie's memories as she talked to me that summer weekend."

Plot Structures and Themes

Somerset Maugham, in *The Art of Fiction*, gives his opinion as to the qualities a good novel should have:

> It should have a widely interesting theme, by which I mean a theme interesting not only to a clique, whether of critics, professors, highbrows, bus-conductors or bartenders, but so broadly human that its appeal is to men and women in general; and the theme should be of enduring interest: the novelist is rash who elects to write on subjects whose interest is merely topical. When they cease to be so, his novel will be as unreadable as last week's newspaper. The story the author has to tell should be coherent and persuasive; it should have a beginning, a middle and an end, and the end should be the natural consequence of the beginning. The episodes should have probability and should not only develop the theme, but grow out of the story.

Let us examine the plot structure and theme of some successful contemporary novels.

The fertile imagination of novelists and their ability to interweave imaginary characters with actual persons is probably best illustrated by *Ragtime,* E. L. Doctorow's best seller. In this novel, Doctorow deals with three completely different personalities: an upper middle class manufacturer, a Jewish silhouette artist, and a Negro jazz pianist. With consummate skill, Doctorow weaves the fortunes of the diverse families of these three people against a background of American life during the years 1912 - 1917 into a complex pattern of varied hues. Their fictional lives interplay with such famous and infamous personages of the time as J. Pierpont Morgan, Evelyn Nesbit, Harry Houdini and Emma Goldman. These historical figures play an active part in the plot.

The novel has its social and political implications: Emma Goldman is a famous radical and feminist; the upper middle class manufacturer is a WASP with many of the prejudices of his class; the black young pianist, Coalhouse Walker, leads an insurrection against injustice. All of these elements are skillfully and entertainingly interwoven.

A novel, as any work of fiction, should entertain. This is not to say that novelists cannot interject social messages. Many novels, such as *Oliver Twist, Uncle Tom's Cabin* and *Black Beauty,* have pleaded for needed societal reforms. The great novels tell an attention-getting story; the message, if there is one, is subtly fused within the story.

H. G. Wells believed that the novel of the future was "to be the social mediator, the vehicle of understanding, the instrument of self-examination, the parade of morals and the exchange of manners, the factory of customs, the criticism of laws and institutions and of social dogmas and ideas." But Somerset Maugham called Wells a propaganidst. Maugham commented, "What it all comes down to is the question whether the novel is a form of art or not. Is its aim to instruct or to please? If its aim is to instruct, then it is not a form of art. For the aim of art is to please. On this poets, painters and philosophers are agreed."

There has been some discourse on basic plots. If we are to arrive at any consensus, it is that there are three major categories: the individual against another individual, the individual against society, the individual against nature. These three categories can be subdivided ad infinitum. Most serious novels deal with the human condition, the interrelationships of men and women. Such a novel is Larry McMurtry's *Terms of Endearment.* McMurtry is the author of *Horseman Pass By* (made into a motion picture under the title of *Hud*) and *The Last Picture Show* (also a highly successful movie). *Terms of Endearment* is structured around the extraordinary character of Aurora Greenway, a middle-aged widow and her varied suitors.

121

Although there is a great deal of comedy in the byplay between Aurora and her suitors, the novel has a serious subplot involving the relations between Mrs. Greenway and her daughter, Emma. At first, there is deep antagonism between mother and daughter. Emma is the antithesis of her vibrant mother. The daughter is unhappy in her marriage to an inept husband. During the course of the novel, Emma matures slowly and finally develops the strength of her mother. It is this strength that brings the two women together and gives the novel its title.

McMurtry merged comedy and pathos, interweaving the passions and the naivete of Aurora's suitors with the poignancy of the mother-daughter relationship. It is basically a novel of characterization rather than situation.

When Toni Morrison wrote her novel, *Sula,* the story of a black woman and a black community, it could easily have been turned into a social tract, but Morrison, being the excellent writer she is, gave us first and foremost a story.

The novel begins in 1919 in the town of Medallion, Ohio, and recounts the events occurring in a black neighborhood. Sula Peace, whose name belies the emotions she stirs in the community, is a close friend of Nel Wright. As youngsters they are involved in the drowning of a little boy. There is not proof of their guilt, but the rumors abound that Sula was responsible, that she is the embodiment of evil. When her mother is burned to death because of an unfortunate accident, Sula stands, unmoved, watching her mother die. After her mother's death, Sula leaves Medallion. She returns some ten years later and renews her friendship with Nel who is now married to Jude Green. But then Nel discovers Sula and Jude making love.

Nel leaves his wife and goes to live with Sula. Sula is not the sort of woman who wants to settle down with one man. She has affairs with other men in town, black and white. By the time she dies in 1941, she is hated by everyone in Medallion.

There are scenes in the novel dealing with racism, particularly the sequence when Nel is taken by train for a visit to New Orleans and suffers the humiliation of segregation.

In *Sula,* Toni Morrison employs what we may term the *catalyst* technique, that is, showing how one person disrupts relationships and, by doing so, destroys the placidity of a community.

Establishing Scenes

The above subheading is borrowed from another medium: motion pictures. If you have ever tried to write a screenplay or seen a copy of a screenplay or a television drama, you may have noted that the opening visual sequence is stated as the *establishing shot.* It is the first picture you see. If the location is a suburb, there are scenes of suburban homes; if the location is Hawaii, the opening may be a long shot of the ocean and surfers. Many novelists begin their stories with that sort of *establishing scene.*

This is how John Fowles begins *The French Lieutenant's Woman:*

> An easterly is the most disagreeable wind in Lyme Bay — Lyme Bay being that largest bite from the underside of England's outstretched leg — and a person of curiosity could at once have deduced several strong probabilities about the pair who began to walk down the quay at Lyme Regis, the small but ancient eponym of the inbite, one incisively sharp and blustery morning in the late March of 1867.
>
> The Cobb has invited what familiarity breeds for at least seven hundred years, and the real Lymers will never see much more to it than a long claw of old gray wall that flexes itself against the sea. In fact, since it lies well apart from the main town, A tiny Piraeus to a microscopic Athens, they seem almost to turn their backs on it. Certainly, it has cost them enough in repairs through the centuries to justify a certain resentment. But to a less tax-paying, or more discriminating, eye it is quite simply the most beautiful sea rampart on the south coast of England.

If it appears to you that this establishing scene seems leisurely in its approach, consider that novels are lengthy, that when you sit down to read a novel, it may take hours or weeks to complete it, depending on how engrossing the book is and how much time you have to devote to reading it. In other words, unlike a short story, you expect to spend a good deal of time with a novel; and its slower pacing, compared to that of the short story, may not be a detriment. This does not by any means imply that dull passages in a novel are acceptable. Quite the contrary is true. But reading a well-written novel may be likened to walking through a botanical garden where you have time to savor and admire the varied and remarkable blossoms.

Pacing

Not only should the threads of the novel be varied, so should its pacing. If the novel is a comedy, there could be a sobering chapter or two. If it is a suspense story, the writer may wish to have an intervening chapter of some placidity as a contrast to the tension. If it is a tragedy, there may be some humor interspread. For example, Chapter Nine of *A Farewell to Arms* is a grim portrayal of war. Frederic Henry, the protagonist and narrator, is a young American attached to an Italian ambulance unit during World War I. He is severely wounded. An Italian comrade is killed. But Chapter Ten finds Henry in a field hospital, and there are scenes with witty and ironic dialogue between Henry and an Italian doctor.

Consider a philosophical analogy. Happiness is relative. If we never know sadness, how can we define happiness? Suspense is heightened if it follows a scene of tranquility. Contrast adds to both the believability and the interest of your story. Dickens wrote, "It was the best of times. It was the worst of times." In our lives we have best times and worst times. A day of joy is heightened even more if it comes after a day of depression.

Think consciously of pacing your novel. After you have written a great deal, pacing will come instinctively.

Chapters

Some novels are written without the chapter format. For example, *Portnoy's Complaint* by Philip Roth has no numbered chapters. Roth, instead, uses headings such as "The Most unforgettable Character I've Met" and "The Jewish Blues." They sound like titles for short stories. But Roth has a rationale. His protagonist, Alexander Portnoy, recites his emotional problems to an analyst throughout the book, so the novel has that sort of running continuity: Portnoy revealing his guilts and fears. The story lends itself to a deviation from the standard chapter format.

There is no fixed rule for chapter divisions, but most novels do employ a standard procedure. There is a reason. Chapters are to the novelist, or should be, what curtain scenes are to the playwright. Wherever possible, it is effective to have each chapter end with some intriguing statement or incident that will impel the reader to turn the page and read on. Mickey Spillane once noted, "The first chapter sells the book. The last chapter sells the next book."

As an illustration, here is the conclusion of Chapter One of Daphne du Maurier's novel *Rule Brittania.*

> She went upstairs slowly, disliking her mission, for untoward events, unless expressly designed to suit the purpose of the doyene, could have unfortunate consequences for the household. She paused at the head of the stairs. The notice "Don't Disturb," which hung from the handle of the door, had been turned around to reveal its reverse. This was the quote from Dante's *Inferno,* "All hope abandon, ye who enter here," which one of Mad's leading men, in days long past, had stuck outside her dressing room as a warning to intruders.
>
> Emma coughed, knocked and went into her grandmother's bedroom.

Titles

How important is a title? For a first novel, it may be very important. The next time you enter a bookstore, note what catches your eye. Chances are that a famous author's name will attract you first: Updike, Irving, Michener. Therefore, a first novel by an unknown author would do well to have an intriguing title.

Marilyn Durham relates that she had titled her first novel *The Man Who Loved Catherine Dancing,* which sounds like just another romance. Her editor changed the title to *The Man Who Loved Cat Dancing,* which gave the title some ambiguity and evidently was effective in arousing the curiosity of the book buyer.

Good reviews, of course, will do more than any title to sell a book. Nevertheless, "the title bout" is something you should spend some time training for. Remember that a good title may be both brief and clear. It should be catchy and to the point. A brief catchy title usually has more impact on a reader. Sometimes, just one word can be a compelling title if it is the right word. Consider the success of such books as *Wheels* by Arthur Hailey, *Jaws* by Peter Benchley and *Deliverance* by James Dickey.

This is not to say that what sounds like an uninspired title will hinder sales. *The Other, Peyton Place, The Thorn Birds* and *Coma* may seem like unimaginative titles for books, but those books became best sellers thanks to word-of-mouth advertising. However, it is possible they may have done even better if they had more intriguing titles.

I suggest to beginning novelists that they not waste time pondering a title before they begin their book. Use any working title. Time enough to consider a title when you complete the book. That's the all-important task before you: complete what you have started. Titles will often jump at you from the pages of your manuscript. Or you may rummage through Bartlett's for a pertinent quotation. *For Whom the Bell Tolls,* for example, was taken from a very old poem by John Donne.

Juvenile

One of my students made the observation that a children's book must appeal to adults. It is a pragmatic observation. Adults buy books for children. Parents browse through bookstores for children's birthday gifts, and when they find themselves enchanted by a story, they buy it. I loved *Charlotte's Web* and so did my children.

I believe the above rationale is correct. Therefore, many of the same elements that make an adult book successful also apply to preparing a juvenile book. Based on my experience with students who want to write for children, I have found that many of them write lovely descriptions that lend themselves to colorful illustrations, but the actual stories lack action. Children want *something to happen* in their stories as much as adults do.

First, I must point out that whereas an adult novel can reach an audience from ages 17 to 70, juvenile books must be targeted to specific age groups.

From ages three to six, we have the preschoolers. They do not read or, at best, if they have parents who are as attentive as they should be, the children are just beginning to read. These youngsters have a short attention span. Books for them should be brief, perhaps not more than a thousand words, and contain numerous illustrations. Preschoolers will pick up a book and be fascinated by the illustrations. However, when adults read books to them the stories must have an exciting incident or two or else the children will become bored. Think of that classic children's story, *The Little Engine That Could.* Remember how that engine huffed and puffed and exerted all its power until it finally got over the mountain. That event illustrates another point: there should be a satisfactory resolution to the children's story.

You need not strive for in-depth character development for the preschoolers. Illustrations are important to them so that they can identify with the child portrayed in the illustrations. These children have a very lively imagination. They love pets and they often converse with them. They, therefore, will accept and relish stories in which animals speak.

Just the mention of illustrations may make some writers think they must also be illustrators or find an illustrator to collaborate. This is not so. Obviously if you can illustrate as well as write, it is an advantage. But not many writers of juveniles are of the caliber of Dr. Seuss or Maurice Sendak. If you have a salable story, the publisher will arrange for an artist to create the illustrations.

For older children, the text is longer and the illustrations are fewer. Children in the six to eight age group have begun to read. Their attention span is longer. Stories for them may run anywhere from two to four thousand words, and although books geared for this age group should be easy to read, the children should not be written down to. Words new to them help increase a child's vocabulary.

For the six to eight group, the fictional characters may be somewhat one-dimensional, that is, they are endowed with a particular characteristic: fun-loving, friendly, studious, stubborn or some other individual quality. There is little change in the character as the story progresses.

The next age group, eight to twelve, includes the most avid readers. Any type of story appeals to them as long as there is a good deal of action. Do not confuse action with violence. Action involves the posing of a problem and the resolution of that problem. The ardent readers of this group will look forward to books that deal with conflicts affecting their peers. They will be interested in more fully developed characters.

Teenagers between thirteen and fifteen have achieved some sophistication. They look for serious stories that encompass problems which concern their peers. Whatever your assessment of television and its influence, the fact is that youngsters do watch a great deal of television and because they do, they are more aware of adult relationships. They may watch news programs and thus also become cognizant of political crises and civic problems. If you plan to write stories for young people in this age group, then consider comtemporary problems that involve teenagers. For these young adults, writers will need to present multidimensional characters much as those in a well written adult novel. Fiction for teenagers will follow the same guidelines as fiction for adults, with one basic difference: the protagonist of the novel for teenagers should be a teenager. Romance, which is not an ingredient for younger children, can be a staple for the teen novel. However, explicit sex scenes should be avoided.

We have specified certain age groups, but these groupings may overlap; for example, some ten-year-olds may enjoy the same books as some thirteen-year-olds.

There is also an area of juvenile books which we may term motivational. They are written for children who read below their age or grade level. These youngsters need to be greatly motivated to read. The stories that will appeal to them contain a good deal of action and suspense. Books for these slow readers may run anywhere from 8,000 to 12,000 words, and should be written in short sentences which are easily understood.

For study purposes, I recommend that you refer to *Best Books for Children,* published by R. R. Bowker.

THE NOVELLA

The novella or short novel usually runs between 25,000 and 50,000 words. It is not a very popular form today, although magazines such as *Redbook* occasionally publish short novels. A few years ago, Harvard University sponsored the publication of novellas to help revive the form, but without any significant success. However, the vagaries of the publishing world and the tastes of the public are often unpredictable, so there is no telling whether a revival may be in the offing.

Because of its brevity compared to the novel, the novella is a very challenging medium. In succinct form, it has all the scope of a novel. As Professor Ray J. Sherer observed in his compilation of *Twelve Short Novels* (Holt, Rinehart and Winston), "while short stories are only expected to provide something like miniature pictures of life, short novels generally share with their full-length counterparts the ambition of creating whole, self-contained worlds of fiction."

The guidelines we have given you for the short story and the novel (with respect to characterization, motivation and so forth) can be used to good advantage in writing the novella.

As with the short story and the novel, writers should familiarize themselves with outstanding examples of the novella, such as *Pale Horse, Pale Rider* by Katherine Anne Porter, *Seize the Day* by Saul Bellow, *The Red Pony* by John Steinbeck and *The Call of the Wild* by Jack London.

— Stanley Field

CHAPTER EIGHT

WRITING FOR TELEVISION, MOVIES AND THE STAGE

The previous chapters of this volume have dealt with the expression of the writer's creativity in print. In considering The audio-visual media, (television, film, state plays and radio), we introduce external requirements to the written word: the camera, scenery, sound effects, music. In our prose creations, we work mainly with an editor. In audio-visual productions, we need producers, directors, actors, composers, musicians, set designers, costume designers, lighting and sound effects specialists.

Writers for audio-visual media must first become familiar with script formats, since they are totally different from the paragraph structure of prose writing.

TELEVISION FORMAT

Writing for television offers some of the greatest opportunities for writers who understand the requirements and needs of this media. First let's take a look at what goes into a television script. On the first page, you will need to list your cast of characters in this manner:

CAST

BELVA LOCKWOOD:	54, a not-unattractive woman of medium height, of great vitality. A widow.
MARTHA DIXON:	Her secretary, about 24. A very personable young woman.
JOHN THUNDERCLOUD:	About 30. He is a half-breed. His father was white, his mother Indian. He is handsome and his

Indian features predominate. He has had an excellent education (Harvard).

The total cast is always listed. The cast identification gives the director an indication of casting requirements.

Your next page should list the number and type of sets required:

SETS

INTERIOR:
Reception Room of Mrs. Lockwood's Law Office
Belva Lockwood's Office
Drawing Room of Mrs. Lockwood's Home
United States Senate Chamber
Stage of an Auditorium

EXTERIOR:
Street Scene

The television play today is either videotaped or filmed. Most of the dramatic productions emanate from Hollywood and a great many of the writers are either current or former screen writers. The format used for the television play is, therefore, a derivative of the motion picture screenplay, as follows:

INTERIOR: DAY
MRS. LOCKWOOD'S living room. MRS. ARCHER and MRS. LOCKWOOD are seated in a pair of upholstered chairs set against the wall. MRS. ARCHER carries a lace handkerchief which she keeps twisting rather nervously. After a moment's pause, she speaks without looking directly at MRS. LOCKWOOD.

MRS. ARCHER

I — well — Mrs. Lockwood, I must confess to you — I do admire you greatly. I've heard so much about you and read so much in the newspapers of you and your accomplishments.

She looks directly now at MRS. LOCKWOOD and her tone becomes belligerent as if someone were prepared to protest.

I think it's wonderful.

MRS. LOCKWOOD

Thank you, Mrs. Archer.

How much technical knowledge should writers have? What should they know about the operation of cameras, scenic design, wide-angle shots, microphone booms, sound effects? Although freelance writers need not immerse themselves in a well of technical terminology, there are some terms with which they should be familiar and which will demonstrate that they are on easy footing with the medium. Directors are responsible for the camera shots. They will indicate, after studying the script, what sort of shots they want. Writers will indicate, on their scripts, descriptions of sets, detailed stage directions, emotional reactions of the actors. Directors often will make changes during rehearsals.

The following definitions are basic examples of television production terms.

ESTABLISHING SHOT: This is the very opening scene of a television play or screenplay. Perhaps your play opens in the kitchen of an average apartment. You might describe the scene as follows:

Example

ESTABLISHING SHOT: The kitchen of the MCLEAN apartment. It is a small kitchen with the usual appliances: a gas stove, a refrigerator, a stainless steel sink, tiled counter tops. There is room for a small table at which the MCLEANS are having breakfast.

TEASER: In television the TEASER is a brief scene preceding the drama. It may be a sequence taken directly from the play or it may be a chronological episode preceding the basic events. It is used to capture the immediate attention of the audience and to prevent it from switching the dial.

TEASER: The chamber of the United States Senate. SENATOR HIRAM ARCHER is in the midst of an harangue.

ARCHER

You may say this woman is a unique person. But I tell you, my dear colleagues, there may be an exodus from our homes. Other women will be emboldened by her victory. Women will want careers for themselves, and motherhood and the family will be destroyed. This year of 1884 will go down in infamy!

DISSOLVE: The DISSOLVE indicates immediate transition. Two scenes will appear on the screen simultaneously for a brief moment until the second scene entirely supersedes the first.

Example

MRS. LOCKWOOD is pacing her office anxiously. Then she sits down at her desk and calls out:

MRS. LOCKWOOD

Martha . . . Martha . . .

DISSOVLE to reception room where MARTHA is besieged by reporters.

FADE-IN: Connotes coming from a blank screen to an ongoing scene.

Example

FADE-IN MARTHA'S office. She is busy at her desk typing.

FADE-OUT: This is the reverse of FADE-IN, in that you go from an ongoing scene to a blank screen. It is also referred to

133

as "fade to black." The FADE-OUT is always employed as the curtain to mark the end of an act.

Example

Will I ever see you again, Dan?

DAN

I don't know.

JOAN

Don't you love me?

DAN

You know I do.

He embraces her and kisses her.
FADE-OUT

CLOSEUP: (or CU, abbreviated): This direction calls for the camera to move forward so that we obtain a waist high or shoulder high view of an actor. At times, the writer may indicate a BIG CLOSEUP or SUPER CLOSEUP to focus on a particular feature of an individual: the eyes, the mouth, the nose.

Example

ALICE

You know that we need to dramatize our cause. You must run for the presidency.

MRS. LOCKWOOD

I need time to consider it.

ALICE

Very well. I'll expect your answer in a week.

MRS. LOCKWOOD nods. ALICE rises and leaves. CLOSEUP of MRS. LOCKWOOD'S face as she ponders her decision.

LONG SHOT: For the LONG SHOT, the camera is moved back a distance so that the entire setting may be visible. LONG SHOTS are often used for opening scenes so that we may have a full view of a living room or a street.

Example

An outdoor platform on MRS. MONTGOMERY'S estate. A large crowd is gathered. LONG SHOT of the area so that we can see the banner strung across the rear of the platform and the many people seated on benches before the platform.

INTERCUT (or CUT): To INTERCUT is to move instantaneously from the picture on one camera to the picture on another. This type of camera action may be used to obtain an immediate reaction from one character to another character's statement.

Example

A shot is fired. MIKE DOLAN falls to the floor. The camera focuses on DOLAN then CUTS to a reaction shot from MARY, who has fired the gun.

SPLIT SCREEN: In utilizing the SPLIT SCREEN device, two cameras are semi-masked so that each image occupies only half the screen.

Example

SARA is seated on the couch in her living room. She has a book in her lap but cannot concentrate on it. She is evidently nervous.

SOUND: The telephone rings.

SARA rushes to answer it. We see her image on screen left. MIKE'S image on screen right.

135

PAN: The panoramic (or PAN) shot affords the audience a view of an entire setting. It is generally a LONG SHOT because of the amount of space it covers and it is a horizontal sweep of the camera. If, for example, one of your scenes is a classroom and you wish to show the attitudes of the students, you will indicate that the camera PANS across the room.

TILT: This is a vertical panoramic shot. The camera may shoot up and down a wall to show an unusual design. It may be used to give an impression of height, as though a child is looking up at a man.

SUPERIMPOSE: This device technically focuses the pictures from two cameras onto a single scene. For example: your heroine has written a tearful farewell to her fiance. We see her staring sorrowfully into space, evidently thinking about her lover. At the same time, we see the young man and we hear him reading the letter aloud. "SUPERS" are used effectively in dramas of the supernatural where audiences may see ghostly figures above the living characters.

TELEVISION DRAMA

The television drama is a complex organism. It must have characterization, motivation, plot structure, exposition, transitions, dialogue, pantomime. To blend all these elements into a finite whole takes consummate skill and artistry. You may raise a questioning eyebrow here, for much of the dramatic fare you have seen on TV hardly qualifies as artistic endeavor. But writers will accomplish little or nothing either by demeaning the medium they work for or by setting their sights too low. Let the finest, not the poorest, of the video dramas be your guide and inspiration.

You cannot plunge into the writing of TV dramas without adequate preparation and study. It is true, and it has happened on occasion, that a writer has watched two or three dramas on the air and then gone to the typewriter to turn out an immediately salable script. But this is the very rare exception, and even in one case when it did occur, the fortunate writer had had a great deal of experience in allied fields. The able video dramatists are both dreamers and practical craftsmen. Their imagination may roam the heavens, but they are fully aware of the down-to-earth requirements of a highly technical medium.

When you watch an adroitly written TV play, you sense that it flows smoothly. Your attention is held by the sweep of the drama. You are unaware of the techniques of the play. After it is over, you may say to yourself, as a viewer, it was well done. As a potential video dramatist, you should be asking why.

You may find, when you write your first TV drama, that you are very conscious of technique. You will be thinking overtly of exposition, of transitions, of the detailed mechanics of your teleplay. This is all as it should be. With experience, these techniques will become automatic. But in order for them to become automatic, you must learn the fundamentals of your craft thoroughly.

Gore Vidal remarked in a magazine article that the television playwright was going to develop a new art form which would, in time, replace the novel, just as the novel had previously replaced poetry.

Television playwrights have not developed a new art form; they are only using a new medium. The television play can trace its forebears to the ancient Greek drama. The basic principles of good drama are as inherent in the television play as they are in the stage play. It will be helpful for aspiring TV playwrights to familiarize themselves with the great classic plays and with the better products of our contemporary theatre.

We also suggest that you refer to our chapter on writing fiction: the basic elements that comprise a successful novel are also essential for the writing of a successful play, whether for tele-vision, the stage or the screen. Nevertheless, we will discuss these elements in this chapter with emphasis on the audio-visual media.

Theme

A play is not a sermon. The serious play does have a message, however, in the sense that the dramatist has something to say to the audience.

You may quite deliberately choose a theme or it may reach you in a burst of inspiration. Many years ago Reginald Rose wrote a very successful TV play, "Twelve Angry Men." It was also made into a memorable motion picture. The theme of the play came to Rose after he had served as a juror and had become aware of a juror's responsibility.

But the playwright cannot be so carried away by the theme, by a personal conviction, that the theme dominates the story. First and foremost, you must have a story to tell and that story must be entertaining and engrossing.

Your theme, on the other hand, may be a very simple one, with no earth-shaking pretensions. You may want to write a love story about Sue and Harry. She is in her early twenties. He is in his fifties. Your theme poses the question: can a marriage be successful when there is a great disparity in age between the bride and groom? It's a familiar theme, but you intend to give it a new twist.

At times, your theme will come after your story. You may want to write a play about your maiden aunt, Sarah. She's really a lively old character, and as you plan your story, you suddenly find yourself with a theme: a spinster's adjustment to life.

Whatever your theme, understatement is preferable to overstatement.

Plot Structure

In the beginning, you either have a situation or you have a character. This is the foundation of your plot structure. You begin to build by putting the proper characters into the situation or inventing a plausible situation for your characters.

You will find a blueprint essential before you proceed. This is your plot outline in which, with more or less detail, you sketch the various scenes. You will have to know, of course, whether your format is intended to be a half-hour situation comedy or perhaps an hour or maybe even a two-hour "made for television" movie. The amount of detail with which you can fill out your plot will depend on the time allotment. Your plot outline should also give you a good indication as to whether you have too many or too few scenes. The one will tend to make your play too episodic, the other too static.

There are certain fundamental principles which are unique to television and of which the playwright must be aware:

The Opening

You must establish interest as quickly as possible. The non-captive audience is in control. Viewers can, by the flick of a switch, turn off your presentation. Therefore, the well-planned play will have an opening incident which will quickly set up the conflict.

Development of Conflict

Each scene of your play, whether written in chronological sequence or with interjected flashbacks, should heighten the conflict. We call this "moving the play." Therefore, if you have a scene which does not move your play, it very likely is unnecessary. If you have any doubt about a scene which you have included, test it by eliminating it from your script. See whether the action of your play is clear without it. Is the sequence essential to the support of your plot, or is it just decorative? You may have written it with loving care and you would hate to delete it because it adds so much color. But because you are always up against the element of time, your decision must always favor the essentials. It is not that these essentials should be bare, but you do not have the scope of a novel in a video play. Novelists may permit themselves the luxury of a four-page description of a farmyard. They may include minute details so that the completed manuscript numbers eight-hundred pages, or they may write tightly-compressed novels in fewer than two-hundred pages. The video dramatist has no such leeway. Time is of the essence.

Curtain Scenes

The television dramatist faces a problem with curtain scenes which is not a problem for the stage or screen playwright. It's the problem of commercial intrusion.

The next time you view a ninety-minute production on a commercial network, keep a watch in hand and time the commercial breaks. If you time several of these programs, you will note that there is a pattern. The opening scene may run 15 or 20 minutes before a commercial break. This is to create substantial interest in the viewer. The playwright has to build this opening to an effective curtain scene so that the audience will stay with the play and even sit through the commercial. Remember that the commercial networks make their profits from advertising; so, all productions have to be geared to the commercials.

As the production continues, note that the time between commercials becomes smaller and smaller until, toward the close of the play, the time between commercials may not be more than five minutes. There is a great burden on the TV playwright to plan his play with these commercial breaks constantly in mind.

Subplots

The insertion of subplots, in which a second story line is also being told, depends on the length of the video drama. The half-hour drama generally does not permit any subplot. The sixty-minute, ninety-minute and two-hour plays do allow for subplots.

Dialogue

Dialogue is the prime mover of the drama. It is possible to present a drama purely in pantomime, but this is not the norm, for speech is normal to people and it is primarily through speech that our thoughts are conveyed in our daily living. In the television drama, dialogue is aided and abetted by visual action.

Dialogue in drama must not only convey information, it must depict emotion. If it lacks emotion, it has no power to hold our attention. The skill of the dramatist reveals itself in the ability to combine these two elements of dialogue: information and emotion. However, the playwright may often have to qualify the emotional content of a line of dialogue since the same line may have many different meanings.

For example, in the following brief scene, the father has just returned from work. He meets his boy in front of their home. He asks about the boxing tournament in which his son participated at the Boys Club.

140

FATHER

How'd you come out in the boxing tournament, son?

SON

I won.

FATHER

Good for you. That makes you champion of the club,
doesn't it?

SON

(DEPRESSED) I guess so.

FATHER

(STUDIES HIS SON ANXIOUSLY) You're not hurt?

SON

Not from any punching, Dad.

FATHER

I see. (GENTLY) Tell me what happened, son.

The son's response, "I guess so," could have been made with
some modesty, but happily, which would indicate that he was
glad to have won the decision. However, the emotional quality
indicated is that of depression, and that informs us that
something must be troubling the boy. No youngster would
normally sound depressed about winning at something.

You will note that in response to his father's question, "You're
not hurt?" the boy replies, "Not from any punching, Dad." No
emotional qualification is needed for this line. The line implies
that he is hurt but not physically. Had the boy merely answered
"No," a qualification would have been needed. An unemotional
"No" would merely indicate that the boy was not hurt physically,
without other implications. However, even the "No," properly
expressed by the actor, could convey the desired emotion.

Characterization by Dialogue

You have probably read a critique or heard someone say that this or that dramatist has a "good ear for dialogue." When Paddy Chayefsky was writing television plays, the comment was made the he might have followed his characters with a tape recorder. As the jacket blurb for Chayefsky's *Television Plays* states: "The author brings these people startlingly close to the reader by means of dialogue that captures the precise nuance of speech and, at the same time, reveals the most secret levels of character." These are objectives of dialogue. But they are objectives not easily attained.

The beginner often has difficulty keeping his characters in character. When this happens, the fault may lie in the fact that the characters are not complete entities in the writer's mind. You can try a simple test with any script on which you are working. Transpose the lines from one character to another. If it appears that each character could just as easily have been given the lines of the other, then the dialogue has failed in one of its most important functions: to create and reveal character.

Think of your friends, your relatives, acquaintances, fellow employees, teachers, the milkman, the postman, the boy who delivers your newspaper. Listen to them speak. Attune your ear to their natural dialogue. Each individual has an idiosyncrasy of speech. Some vary slightly. Some vary greatly. But remember, each is an individual and you want to create individuals.

You may need to exaggerate to some extent a speech peculiarity of a character. This will have the effect of indelibly stamping the character in the minds of the viewers. However, you must be careful not to turn your character into a caricature by overexaggeration.

In delineating character, you may use both a direct and an indirect approach.

Direct: (a) The character describing herself:

MRS. DIXON

Henry, you're wonderfully persistent and I adore you for it. But I really would be hard to live with. I've had to fight all my life. When I was left a widow, and Martha just a baby then, I had to struggle for a living. I remember how I fought with the Board of Trustees to have them pay me the same wages as the men teachers. Everywhere I went, they were prejudiced against me because I had to work, and they penalized me because I was a woman.

(b) Delineation of the character by another with whom she is in conversation:

WOODSON

You're tired, Clara. I mustn't keep you any longer.

MRS. DIXON

No, Henry, please sit down. Just a few minutes longer. Sometimes I think I ought to be like any other woman of my generation . . . like Donna, perhaps. I imagine it would make life so much simpler. But I can't, Henry, I can't.

WOODSON

Of course not. You're Clara Dixon . . . a woman of great ambition . . . of high ideals . . . and probably very hard to live with. But I'm willing to chance all that.

Indirect: Two characters describing a third:

MRS. ANDERSON

Clara's such a remarkable woman. I believe she's the most brilliant woman I've ever known. And so daring. Don't you think so, Dr. Woodson?

WOODSON

I do, indeed.

Thus, we have actually three different approaches in the use of dialogue to delineate character. The portrait of Clara Dixon is not the work of one painter for there are many who have sketched her and, indeed, she has added a self-portrait.

Selectivity

Because of the arbitrary time limits of television drama, dialogue must be highly selective. Each line should have some bearing on the progression of the play. You can make another test for yourself by eliminating any dialogue of which you are not sure. If the story line remains clear, if no necessary information is deleted, then, in all probability, the lines are superfluous. The experienced televison playwright has learned the value of words and has acquired the ability to choose those which tell the most in the least time.

Pantomime

The next time you take a walk through your neighborhood, observe the reactions of people meeting each other. Do they smile? Do they shake hands vigorously? Do they pass each other by with a curt nod? Do they embrace? Do they seem embarrassed?

Jot down a few notes describing your reactions. You think these two people like each other; you think the other two are rather unfriendly. In other words, the physical reactions of people to each other are informative. Even the lack of emotion is enlightening. It tells you the individual is a cold fish, or inhibited or very placid.

Thus, the emotional reactions of your characters, their facial expressions, their gestures, in effect, become another tool for characterization and for exposition. Suppose you are writing a crime drama. You have a scene where the heroine is in her room alone. There is a knock at the door. She goes to open it. A man enters. She steps back, her face contorted in fright. The pantomime is revelatory. It informs you that she is afraid of the man. The dialogue will tell you why.

The pantomime the dramatist indicates for his play must be as much in keeping with the characters as the dialogue. The physical reactions of an elderly person will differ from those of a youth. The environment which has helped to mold your characters will also influence their reactions. A young woman

144

reared in luxury may manifest her distaste if suddenly brought into an ancient tenement. Her facial expression of disgust or displeasure may be her first outward reaction.

The question as to how visual your video drama ought to be depends entirely on the type of play. A western or adventure drama may be mostly visual. A drawing room comedy will depend, most likely, on the dialogue. Pantomime can be used whenever action alone can tell the story.

Exposition

One of the challenges confronting the dramatist is the problem of exposition. Time is limited. Since writers have been told repeatedly that every line of dialogue and every action must advance the play, they sometimes feel at an impasse when faced by the necessity of providing details. How do they explain the relationship of their characters? How can a new character be introduced? How can the time period of the play be established?

All these elements are necessary in order to present a coherent story. Viewers are not apt to be absorbed in a play which frequently confuses them. Yet the exposition must not be self-evident. As a lovely gown conceals its stitching, so must a well-made play veil its mechanics.

There are at least three tools writers can use to provide needed information:

1. Monologues
2. Dialogues
3. Sets and Costumes

Monologue

In utilizing monologue, the writer may employ a narrator to set the scene, to explain the passage of time and to comment on the action. This is the simplest and most direct way of handling exposition. Although the device of the narrator may present less of a challenge to the writer, there are instances where the narrative technique may serve very effectively.

145

MACCABEE

My name is Doctor Joshua Maccabee and I speak to you out of the centuries. The year was seventeen-twenty-one. My wife, my daughter and I took passage on the sailing vessel, *Great Hope,* leaving from London for the New World, where we hoped to find freedom, and a new life.

Dialogue

The most effective method of incorporating the necessary exposition in your play is to use dialogue. The natural flow of conversation should perform the double duty of carrying along the play and including necessary explanatory details.

Example

FADE IN:

INTERIOR — DAY. A small, neighborhood grocery store. An elderly man is behind the counter. The door opens and a young man enters. He walks up to the counter.

YOUNG MAN

Hello, Pa.

As you see, there are no more than two words of dialogue but immediately they inform the audience of the relationship of the two characters: father and son. Had the writer merely written, "Hello," it would have taken at least another line of dialogue or perhaps a few more to establish the relationship. The fact is that since the television writer always has to be conscious of time, every line should have its value. Exposition, especially, requires a maximum of information with a minimum of wordage.

Sets and Costumes

The physical scenes themselves may be valuable aids to exposition. Writers may go into fairly elaborate detail in describing the various sets of their plays and the costumes of the cast. They may choose instead to use just a few explanatory lines and leave the details to the scenic designer.

A scene description may be as simple as this:

FADE IN:

1. INT. DAY -

The dining room of JUNE FOSTER'S home, a typical room of a typical middle income suburban home.

Or writers may elaborate:

FADE IN:

1. INT. NIGHT -

The kitchen-dining room of the BLEAKER flat. Its poverty is all too evident, from the ancient wheezy refrigerator and the equally ancient gas stove to the walls sadly in need of paint. A large round table, one of whose legs is wobbly, stands in the center of the large room. There are a half-dozen hard-backed chairs around the table. A worn oilcloth serves as a tablecloth. The room is poorly lit, as if the light bulbs were of a smaller size than necessary. MRS. MARY BLEAKER is at the stove. A soup pot is being heated. She is of medium height, thin and peaked. She is in her early forties but looks much older. She wears a worn apron and is stirring the soup with a wooden ladle.

Whether the scene description is brief or detailed, the writer should be sure to indicate any properties essential to the plot.

The Flashback

The flashback is a device for portraying an episode of the past which bears a relation to the current action of a play. It can be very effective if used skillfully and sparingly. However, it is important for the writer who wishes to utilize this device to be aware of the technicalities involved.

147

The viewer is accustomed to seeing progressive action. It is also easier to follow a play that moves forward in a straight line. If you have ever watched or listened to a daily serial, you may have observed that the flashback is rarely, if ever, employed. It is also true that most television dramas, whether one-shot or series, use the flashback only occasionally. Nevertheless, there are times when the writer finds that the flashback is extremely helpful to a play.

Since the flashback is a retrogression in time, it requires special handling. The viewer must be prepared for this backward look.

In order that the flashback sequence take place smoothly, the camera must be put to most effective use. One common method is to have the camera go out of focus so that the screen is blurred and it achieves a sort of mystical effect preparing the viewer for a very different sort of sequence. When the camera comes back into focus, the viewers are now in the past. This effect is called *defocusing.* The process is repeated in returning from the past to the present action.

Another device is *matching dissolves.* If the story is about an old charwoman who had known better days, there might be a scene of the old woman down on her knees scrubbing the floor of a deserted office. The camera might focus on her weary, gnarled hands; then there is a slow dissolve and we see another pair of hands, young, immaculate, lovely. They are the hands of the charwoman when she was a teenager.

The following is an example of a flashback:

FADE IN:

1. EXTERIOR — NIGHT

A foxhole on a Korean hill, CORPORAL MATT HERKIMER is on sentry duty . . . a lonely vigil. Sometimes stabs of light tear across the darkness and the rumble of artillery is heard in the distance. Then it is quiet. We can make out CORP. HERKIMER'S face dimly. He is about 23, but his face has that mature seriousness about it which young men acquire who have gone through the hell of combat. His carbine is

148

gripped in his hands as he sits in the foxhole. He stares out into the night and we can hear his thoughts.

MATT

(RECORDED)

Wish I could smoke. Better not. In this darkness it'd be like a beacon. A match'd' flare up
like that light. Well, it won't be long now. I'll
be goin' home, leavin' these black ridges of
Korea . . . the back breakin' hills of Korea . . .
the smell of the valleys. Home to the Blue
Ridges of Virginia . . . the clean, sweet air of
the Shenandoah valley.

2. The camera moves back so that MATT is no longer
visible. We see only the background and the stabs of
light in the distance, but we still hear MATT'S voice.

And the nights, blue and bright with a million
stars. Remember, Elly? . . . It was Saturday
night and we were just comin' out of the
movies. Jim and Claire were ahead of us.

3. DEFOCUS — FADE OUT

FADE IN:

4. EXT. — NIGHT

Front of movie house. The marquee is barely visible.
JIM and CLAIRE come on frame as if exiting from
movie. They stand before entrance and wait.

JIM

(LOOKS BACK) What happened to Matt and
Elly?

CLAIRE

If you can remember, Jim, before we were
married, we used to walk very slowly, too, arm
in arm.

MATT

Coming on, holding tightly on ELLY'S arm. It is June
and he wears an open shirt. ELLY wears a summer
dress with a star pattern. She leans against MATT as
they stop beside JIM and CLAIRE.

That was a pretty good show, don't you think
so, Jim?

A Footnote

Unlike the novelist, short story writer and poet who speak
directly to their audience, television playwrights must reach their
audience through a host of interpreters.

The play, like music, requires performance. Although it is true
that a play may be read with a great deal of enjoyment and benefit
to the reader, even so, the play has been written to be acted out.
Full satisfaction can only come about with a competent performance. The playwright, however, must never lean on the
performer. Characterizations must be full-blown. A great
performer may possibly transcend inadequate writing, but with
all due respect to our talented stars, the drama is basic.

MARKETING

Although television's need for playscripts is monumental, it is
difficult for the new writer to break in. You may submit a short
story, unsolicited, to a magazine. Some publishers (particularly,
the smaller ones) will read unsolicited book manuscripts. But for
television scripts, with hardly any exception, you will need an
agent. You may query literary agents to see whether they would
be interested in handling TV scripts. Additionally, you should
check the *Literary Marketplace* for names of agents whose
offices are in Los Angeles. If you have any contacts at all, even a

150

secretary who works for a producing firm, use them. You may contact the programming department of the networks to see whether they might be interested in reading your TV play. If, by any chance, they are, they will send you a release to sign before submitting your play. The release entirely favors the network, but you won't get a reading unless you sign it.

Years ago, there were many play anthologies on the networks, so there was a constant market for new plays. Today, almost all the dramas are series: situation comedies, crime, adventure, romance, fantasy. You usually need to write a script based on the characters of a particular series.

Copyright

It is recommended that you copyright or register any of your playscripts. Applications for copyrights may be obtained by writing to the Copyright Office, The Library of Congress, Washington, D.C. 20540. Or you may register scripts with the Writer's Guild of America, East, 1212 Avenue of the Americas, New York, New York 10036 or Writer's Guild of America, West, 8955 Beverly Boulevard, Los Angeles, California 90048.

Public Broadcasting

In some instances, local Public TV stations have fostered new dramatists. In the main, Public stations have budget difficulties. Dramatic programs such as *The American Short Story* on PBS are financed by grants. If you have a comparable series in mind, you can write to the Program Officer/Media, National Endowment for the Humanities, Washington, D.C. 20506 and ask for information on submitting proposals.

Cable

Cable may be the wave of the future. Already some independent producing firms in addition to the major producers and the networks are planning programs for the expanding cable television and this may open new opportunities for writers.

THE DOCUMENTARY

The documentary might well be called the conscience of the broadcasting industry. Within its scope, causes have been fought, problems analyzed, issues dramatically portrayed. Whatever its approach, its technique, the documentary deals entirely with facts.

For purposes of this text, we have classified documentaries into three categories: (1) Action; (2) Information; (3) Dramatization.

There is some overlapping in these categories. In any creative field, rules are flexible rather than rigid.

The *Action* documentary portrays a problem of the contemporary scene and shows what can be done about it or editorializes about what should be done about it.

Here is a brief sequence from a documentary script, *Garbage is a Dirty Word,* which I wrote for Stuart Finley Productions:

VISUAL	AUDIO
Truck driving through New York streets	(MUSIC) In New York City, civic minded people have banded together in the Environmental Action Coalition to combat all the elements in our daily lives which cause pollution.
School children packing newspapers into truck	(MUSIC) The Coalition motivates school children to gather newspapers for resale and recycling. It has a Volunteer Speakers Bureau which provides information to schools and community groups on environmental problems.

This *Action* documentary was presented on many TV stations around the country. Its purpose was to get communities concerned about cleaning up their environment.

Note that the format is quite different from a playscript. For this documentary I was writing against available film footage and therefore the narration had to be tailored to the film.

Many documentaries have scenarios written prior to any shooting. For example, if you were assigned as a writer for a documentary on slum areas, you would need to do extensive research at those areas besides whatever background you needed — historic, statistical, economic. You would then write your script, which the director would use as a shooting guide.

The *Information* documentary is a study in exposition. It could, for example, demonstrate the development of computers and explain in detail how they operate. It could be a medical documentary informing you of the causes and treatments of cancer.

Whereas the *Action* and *Information* documentaries deal with actualities and utilize the actual people who took part in the events, the *Dramatized Documentary* recreates a situation *based* on actuality. For example, a documentary may be produced on the life of General Omar Bradley, using actors to portray the General and all other participants. Actors are not used in all other types of documentaries except as narrators.

Many documentary films use no writers. These documentaries are generally a mix of original footage, stock footage and interviews. They are the province of producers and directors. For example, my daughter, Connie Field, was the producer/director of the multi-award winning documentary film, *The Life and Times of Rosie the Riveter.* The documentary is a compilation of historic film footage showing the "Rosies" at work during World War II, with five "Rosies" telling their stories of how it actually was during those tumultuous days and what has happened to them since then. The film is skillfully edited; but there is no narrator and, therefore, no need for narration. The "Rosies" speak for themselves. This is the method that many independent film producers use today in the presentation of their documentaries.

The Mini-Documentary

In the past decade, we have seen the proliferation of mini-documentaries. These are features usually presented in three to five minute segments on a daily basis during regularly scheduled news broadcasts. Generally, they are investigative in nature, and mostly, they are produced by local TV stations. The subjects covered are both of local and of national interest.

The mini-documentary series for the local TV station takes the place of producing half-hour or hour documentaries which then would have to compete with network programs. By presenting the mini-documentaries within established news programs, a twofold purpose is served: the mini-documentary has a ready-made audience and its investigative nature helps to increase that audience.

THE STAGE

The theatre has spread its wings. Besides Broadway, there are dozens of Off-Broadway theatres. The past two decades also have seen the growth of regional theatres, such as the *Arena* in Washington, D.C. Just about every large city in the United States has small, active civic groups producing plays and looking for playscripts. In addition, dinner theatres are achieving great success. So, if you've been wanting to write a play and wondering whether there is a market — there is.

The principles enunciated in playwriting for TV should be observed in writing for the stage, with some major differences.

The stage play is presented "live." It, therefore, presents a greater challenge to the playwright than writing for film, which is so flexible. Most plays today are written in two acts. Of course there may be several scenes in each act. Whether you do have two full acts, or interspersed scenes, you need to build your plot to a crisis at each scene or at the end of the first act. The curtain will physically come down after each scene and there will be an intermission after the first act.

154

The dialogue in a stage play should be more image-provoking than the screenplay. The tendency on the screen is this: if a character is describing an incident in his or her life to another character, the screen will then flash back visually to that incident. In a stage play, the character will need more vivid dialogue so that the audience will be able to mentally visualize the scene.

The beginning playwright generally faces a tremendous challenge. Play producers are entrepreneurs; that is to say, if they find a play they want to produce, they must scurry about finding investors to back the play. With an unknown playwright, money will be hard to come by. It is therefore advisable for the new playwright to plan his or her play so that it takes place in one setting.

One set will cut costs tremendously. It is also advisable for the new playwright to limit his or her cast. That is not to say that you ought to write a play with two characters. It has been done successfully, but I would hardly advise it for the novice.

We have mentioned the proliferation of play producing groups throughout the country. The Theatre Communications Group publishes a brochure that lists regional theatres and their requirements and also many of the playwriting contests. The cost of the brochure is nominal. You may write to: Publications Department, Theatre Communications Group, 355 Lexington Ave., New York, N.Y. 10017. Ask for the booklet: "Information for Playwrights" and its cost.

EPILOGUE

Although breaking into the audio-visual field is difficult, new writers do all the time. It may be a long struggle, but the rewards can be fabulous both in money and in prestige. If you have the desire, then study the medium, and, above all, have persistence.

— Stanley Field

AFTERWORD

Having now devoted several hours of your time to studying and practicing the writing and marketing skills taught in this book, you are prepared to take the plunge into an active career as a freelance writer. This is not to say that you will meet with immediate success. Everything from learning to tie your shoes to becoming a concert violinist takes time, practice and determination. Surely, finding success as a freelance writer is no less challenging.

Most people who have a burning desire to write need little encouragement. There is something in them that simply *must* get out — a burst of creativity, a personal story or a new theory or idea. They know they will never be content until they have committed these thoughts to paper.

Perhaps you are one of these people. If so, you have learned by now that enthusiasm alone cannot guarantee success as a freelance writer. This knowledge may have even been the factor that led you to read this book.

We are pleased that your desire to become a writer has made you want to learn to create better syntax, construct better paragraphs and develop more realistic characters. This is good. You cannot reach your full writing potential without these and other skills. Nevertheless, you need to maintain your original starry-eyed trust in your enthusiasm.

Your ability to dream and to fabricate illusions of grandeur is and essential ability for your career as a writer. Never be hesitant about imagining forthcoming success. As the song says, "If you don't have a dream, how you gonna make a dream come true?"

When most successful writers begin work on a new book, they set to their task with full confidence that they *will* be successful. Most of these writers can visualize in their imaginations what their printed books will look like once they are written and published. They "see" a successful end product and proceed toward it with excitment and determination. Journalists and short story writers do likewise.

As we bring this book to a close, we would like to offer you some final words of encouragement. In the coming weeks and years, we hope you'll return to this section of our book whenever you feel depressed, weighted down by rejection or in doubt of your abilities. Use these reminders to bolster your spirits:

Remember that *manuscripts get rejected, not authors.* No author ever born sold everything he or she wrote. If a manuscript does not sell, it is a sign of poor timing, inappropriate topic choice or yet-to-be-developed writing skills. Keep trying. A rejected manuscript is not a value judgment of you or your career.

Maintain your writing regimen. Get something on paper. You cannot sell a story or article that is in your head. Write it down. You'll surprise even yourself at how much talent you have.

Never stop learning. Read writers' magazines and textbooks. Attend writers' conferences and workshops. Expand your writing skills at every opportunity. Everything you learn becomes grist for the writing mill.

Preserve and enhance your unique qualities. Be proud of your writing style. Don't copy other authors; offer your own special writing perspective to your readers. No one else can write like you. Capitalize on that.

Enjoy your earnings. Deduct a little "mad money" from each of your royalty checks. You will have earned it. Don't let your writing become strictly a business venture. Have fun with it.

Write on!

Dennis E. Hensley

Stanley Field